GREAT BRITISH PUDDINGS

**OVER 140 SWEET, STICKY, YUMMY, CLASSIC RECIPES
FROM THE WORLD-FAMOUS PUDDING CLUB**

THE
PUDDING CLUB
EST. 1985

EBURY
PRESS

10 9 8 7 6 5 4 3 2 1

Published in 2012 by Ebury Press, an imprint of Ebury Publishing

A Random House Group Company

The Random House Group Limited Reg. No. 954009

Addresses for companies within the Random House Group can be found at
www.randomhouse.co.uk

A CIP catalogue record for this book is available from the British Library

The Random House Group Limited supports The Forest Stewardship
Council® (FSC®), the leading international forest certification
organisation. Our books carrying the FSC label are printed on FSC®
certified paper. FSC is the only forest certification scheme endorsed by the
leading environmental organisations, including Greenpeace. Our paper
procurement policy can be found at www.randomhouse.co.uk/
environment

To buy books by your favourite authors and register for offers visit
www.randomhouse.co.uk

Photographer: Dan Jones
Food stylist: Abi Fawcett
Props stylist: Polly Webb-Wilson
Design and art direction: Smith & Gilmour, London
Copy editor: Ione Walder

Printed and bound in China by C&C Offset Printing Co., Ltd

ISBN 9780091945428

CONTENTS

WHAT IS
THE PUDDING CLUB?

THE PUDDING CLUB was started in the Cotswold village of Mickleton in 1985 by a small but dedicated group of pudding lovers. They were determined not to let the traditional British puddings they loved and craved become extinct as a result of quick-cook convenience foods and overseas influences!

In the autumn of 1985 this small band of aficionados joined together for an evening of indulgence where the stars included seven delicious puddings — childhood favourites like treacle sponge pudding and jam roly poly, which at that time were not widely available. It's hard to believe now but in 1985 they were rarities!

The Pudding Club's heartfelt mission for over a quarter of a century has been to preserve the Great British Pudding. Indeed, this has been achieved on many restaurant and pub menus, and in farm shops and supermarkets up and down the land. The fame of the Great British Pudding is no longer confined to these shores: The Pudding Club has been on tour overseas and has a following in Japan, North America, Belgium, the Netherlands and Ireland, among other places. International visitors come to our little Cotswold village to experience this slightly eccentric institution, and to be able to say that they have taken part in a Pudding Club meeting and even stayed in a pudding-themed bedroom too. Where else can you sleep surrounded by images of syrup sponge or spotted dick and custard?

Guests at Pudding Club meetings enjoy a whole evening's entertainment, from a jovial introduction by the Pudding Master through the Parade of Seven Puddings, with all its noise and ceremony, to the vote for best pudding of the night! Pudding Club meetings have been likened to many things but a couple of comments stay in the memory: 'Like making love in a thunderstorm', a 'medieval banquet with custard', and it has even been described as 'the eighth wonder of the world'. Visitors to a Pudding Club meeting will understand that the evening is about indulgence, fun and being a bit naughty to boot! You too can join in the fun and attend a meeting (see page 224).

Sheila Vincent is the queen of puds in Mickleton, and she's now world-famous too after producing amazing puddings and seven gallons of custard every Friday night for so many years! As for the three of us, we're passionate about puddings and proud to be passing on our treasured recipes to you — we hope you will eat, drink and be merry!

JILL, PETER & SIMON

THE
PUDDING CLUB
EST. 1985

THE GREAT BRITISH PUDDING

Steamed or baked; layered or rolled; scattered with crumble; served hot with custard or cold with cream – the British pudding comes in countless shapes, sizes and styles. Our traditional puddings have become famed the world over.

The history of the British pudding is long and varied. Many recipes can be traced back through the centuries, immortalised in old cookbooks or passed down from one generation to the next. For many of us, a particular pudding can evoke childhood memories or nostalgia for the good-old days. For others, they promise the warmth and comfort of home, of meals shared with loved ones, or lazy Sunday afternoons.

The British pud is currently enjoying a much-deserved revival in popularity, with celebrity chefs and restaurants featuring traditional puddings on their menus. But whilst some recipes have been constantly revived and reinvented, such as our celebratory trifles and famous lemon meringue pie, others have been almost forgotten, such as the Kentish well pudding or apple dappy. This book celebrates them all, combining classics, new twists and lesser-known recipes rescued from the past. So whether you're feeding your family or entertaining guests, splashing out or cooking on a budget, you will find perfect puddings for every occasion.

OUR RECIPES

This book is a collection of recipes that have been served at Pudding Club meetings over the years. From 15th-century recipes, to our contemporary Millennium pudding, they represent a timeline of pudding history. Since our puds are normally much larger (as we serve up to 70 people), each recipe has been adapted for cooking at home and thoroughly updated to use ingredients available today, but still retaining wonderful traditional elements. Most notable is suet, which these days has largely disappeared from British kitchens (aside from its use in dumplings), but many of our puddings would be unrecognisable without it. Vegetable suet is available in any supermarket, whilst fresh beef suet can be bought from most butchers and is very economical. We also encourage you to seek out some of the lesser-used seasonal British fruits, such as damsons, gooseberries, rhubarb and quince – it was for these traditional fruits that many puddings were devised, and we think they deserve to be enjoyed as originally intended.

COOKING TIPS

Because many pudding recipes are prepared, assembled and cooked in similar ways, a number of instructions crop up again and again in the recipes throughout this book. This section outlines some of the most commonly used equipment and techniques.

PUDDING BASINS

A book on British puddings wouldn't be complete without the archetypal steamed variety, with its iconic basin shape. These are among the oldest domestic British puddings – until the 19th century, very few kitchens had ovens, so food had to be boiled or steamed. There are two types of steamed pud: the sponge-based pudding, made like a batter and poured into a greased basin, and those that require suet pastry, which is used to line the basin, producing a crumbly outer crust and dense interior.

In this book we generally use a 1.1 litre (2-pint) basin. Very occasionally we specify a 1.5-litre (2½-pint), 1.7-litre (3-pint) or 2.3-litre (4-pint) basin. Some of our recipes require individual 200ml (7fl oz) basins. If you don't have the necessary size, feel free to improvise by dividing your ingredients between smaller basins or by multiplying the ingredients to fit a larger one, but never fill the basin more than two-thirds full. (If you don't have a pudding basin, you can use a regular bowl, but do make sure it's heatproof and heavy-duty as it will need to withstand several hours submerged in a hot pan of water.) Remember that adjusting the basin size will also affect the cooking time, so check the pudding to determine whether it's properly cooked.

LINING A BASIN WITH PASTRY

Divide the suet pastry into two thirds and one third and set the smaller piece aside. Grease the pudding basin with butter and dust your work surface with flour. Roll out the larger piece of dough into a rough circle and position it inside the greased basin, pressing it snugly against the edges. Add the other ingredients to the pudding as directed in the recipe, then roll out the smaller piece of dough, wet the edges, and place on top, pushing down gently at the edges so that the two pieces of pastry stick to each other.

An alternative lining method is to roll out the whole piece of dough into a circle, then cut away a quarter to save for the lid. Place the larger piece inside the basin, bring the two cut edges together and press them to join. Once you've filled the pudding, re-roll the reserved pastry into a circle that will fit on top and adhere by wetting the edges with water and pushing down, as described above.

COVERING A BASIN

Before steaming, your basin needs to be properly sealed, so that no water can get inside and make the pudding soggy. Nowadays, many pudding basins can be bought with lids. These basins are often plastic. However, if you're using a traditional ceramic basin or any other bowl, it's unlikely to have its own lid, so you'll need to cover the basin with foil and/or greaseproof paper. Ideally, use two layers: one of greaseproof and one of foil. (However, don't worry if you only have one or the other; simply use a double layer of whatever is available.) Cut a large square of each and lay one on top of the other. With the two held together, fold a pleat down the centre to allow space for the pudding to rise.

Put the covering over the basin, positioning the greaseproof nearest to the pudding, the foil outermost and the pleat across the centre, and fold the edges down around the basin. Secure with string, tied just under the rim of the basin, to make the cover watertight. Also tie a loop of string that you can use as a handle to lower the basin in and out of the pan. Trim off any excess foil/greaseproof.

STEAMING A PUDDING

The most basic way to steam a pudding is over a pan of simmering water. If you have a steamer pan with tiers that stack on top of each other, this is ideal. Otherwise, use a large, deep saucepan with a lid. The pudding basin mustn't directly touch the bottom of the pan or it will burn, so you'll need to raise it on a trivet — you can use an upturned saucer, ramekin or scrunched-up disc of foil for this.

Pour enough water into the pan so that it will reach just over halfway up the sides of the basin, then lower the basin onto the trivet and cover the pan with a tight-fitting lid. Bring the water to a steady simmer and steam the pudding for the allotted time. Try to keep the water at around the same level throughout — check regularly and top up with boiling water from the kettle if it looks low (never add cold water). Don't be tempted to unwrap the pudding until it's nearing the end of its cooking time or it may sink.

When ready, use the string handle to raise the basin out of the pan. Cut the string and unwrap the pudding. When cooked, the pudding should be firm to the touch and a skewer inserted into the centre should come out cleanly. If it's not ready, you'll need to re-cover the pudding and steam for a little longer.

It's also possible to steam puddings in an electric steamer and even in a pressure cooker. Some ovens now come with a steamer function. Always refer to the manufacturer's instructions for advice and be prepared that the cooking time may vary from what's stated in the recipe — be sure to check the pudding with a skewer as described above.

To remove a pudding from its basin once cooked, run a sharp knife around the edges, place a serving plate upside down on top of the basin and invert the pudding onto the plate.

BASIC SHORTCRUST PASTRY

Shortcrust pastry forms the base of so many delicious tarts and pies. It's best handled as little as possible, so making it in a food processor is preferable, though instructions are also given for making by hand. Ensure the pastry is rolled out thinly, and these quantities will fit the tins specified, with a small amount left over that you can use for making decorations, or store in the fridge or freezer for another use.

If you prefer a sweeter pastry, the salt can be replaced with a pinch of sugar, but bear in mind that this makes the pastry crumblier and trickier to work with. You can also adapt the pastry by adding grated lemon or orange zest, a pinch of cocoa powder or even seeds from a vanilla pod. Always be sparing, to keep the flavours subtle.

Lines a 20–22cm (8–9in) tart tin (makes 225g/8oz)
130g (4½oz) plain flour
Pinch of salt
65g (2½oz) unsalted butter, chilled
Iced water

Lines a 30cm (12in) tart tin (makes 375g/13oz)
210g (7½oz) plain flour
Pinch of salt
110g (4oz) unsalted butter, chilled
Iced water

SIFT THE FLOUR AND SALT into a food processor (or see below for making by hand). Cut the cold butter into small pieces and drop in on top.

Process for 20–30 seconds, then add ice-cold water, a tablespoon at a time, with the machine still running. You should need 2–3 spoonfuls.

IF THE MIXTURE IS STILL crumbly after a minute or two, add another tablespoon of water, but bear in mind that the more water you add, the more the pastry will shrink when blind baked (adding cream or egg yolk instead of water is a solution to this). Once the pastry has come together into a ball, stop the processor, remove the dough and wrap in cling film. Leave in the fridge for at least 30 minutes before rolling out.

TO MAKE THE PASTRY by hand, sift the flour and salt into a large bowl then add the chopped butter and work as quickly as you can to rub the fat into the flour with your fingertips. Add water as above, then wrap in cling film and chill in the fridge for 30 minutes.

DUST YOUR WORK SURFACE, rolling pin and hands with flour, then start rolling – always away from you, turning the pastry as you go. Keep the rolling pin and work surface floured to prevent sticking. Once rolled out, slip the rolling pin under the top third of the pastry and pick it up and lay over your greased tin or dish. Never stretch it as it will just shrink back. Try to chill the unbaked pastry case in the fridge for at least 30 minutes before use. Depending on the pudding recipe you are following, you may need to blind bake the pastry case (see opposite) before filling it.

LINING A TART TIN

Whether you've made the pastry from scratch or are using store-bought, it should be chilled before you begin. Dust a clean work surface with flour and gently roll out the chilled pastry, rolling away from yourself and turning the pastry at intervals to keep it roughly circular. Roll until the pastry is larger than the diameter of the tart tin and around 5mm (¼in) in thickness. To check it is large enough, place the tart tin gently on top and ensure there is enough excess all the way around to sufficiently line the sides.

Thoroughly grease the tin (if it's fluted, a pastry brush can be helpful for greasing into the creases). Place your rolling pin on top of the rolled-out pastry and loosely roll it up around the pin. Lift the pin up, position it above the tin and unroll the pastry into place. Ensure it is central, with the same amount of excess all the way round.

Gently ease the pastry into the base and sides of the tin, being careful not to tear or dent it with your fingertips. Trim any excess from the edges with a sharp knife, allowing a little bit of extra to account for any shrinking. Prick the base of the pastry with a fork and chill the pastry case in the fridge for up to 30 minutes — this helps to reduce shrinkage. Once chilled, either blind bake (see below) or fill immediately, depending on the pudding recipe you are following.

BLIND BAKING

'Blind baking' is the process of baking an empty tart or pie case before it is filled. It ensures that the base of the pastry is crisp and cooked through and isn't made soggy by the addition of the filling. As directed above, the case should be pricked with a fork and chilled for up to 30 minutes before blind baking.

Preheat the oven to 190°C (400°F), Gas Mark 5. Cut a circle of greaseproof paper or baking parchment and place it inside the pastry case. Fill with baking beans (you can use uncooked rice or lentils as an alternative), spreading them out to evenly cover the base. Bake in the oven for about 15 minutes until the edges are lightly browned. Remove the baking beans and paper and put back in the oven for 10 minutes until the base is cooked. Allow to cool and then fill the case as required.

CHAMPION PUDDINGS

At Pudding Club meetings, we serve up seven different puddings. Once guests have been given the opportunity to try them all (and even come back for seconds!), they are asked to vote for their favourite. The pudding with the most votes is crowned the champion.

The seven puddings in this chapter are the ones that have been voted champion on the most occasions. An irresistible line-up of British classics, they demonstrate how wonderfully varied our sweet fare can be. From indulgent sticky toffee to refreshing summer pudding, there is something here for everyone, whether you prefer your pud hot or cold; steamed or baked; spongy or crisp; creamy, syrupy or fruity...

Bread and butter pudding

SERVES 4-6

120g (4oz) sultanas
1 tbsp brandy (optional)
120–180g (4–6½oz)
  unsalted butter, softened,
  plus extra for greasing
12 slices of white bread,
  crusts removed
Finely grated zest and juice
  of 1 orange
3 eggs
600ml (1 pint) milk
90g (3oz) caster sugar
Ground cinnamon or
  nutmeg, to sprinkle
Custard, to serve (optional)

IF YOU WANT TO SOAK the sultanas in brandy, put them together in a bowl and leave to soak for up to 30 minutes. Grease a 1.1-litre (2-pint) ovenproof baking dish.

BUTTER THE BREAD SLICES on one side. Line the bottom and sides of the greased dish with some of the bread, butter-side up, and sprinkle with half the orange juice and grated zest. Add half the sultanas, followed by another layer of bread, then the remaining sultanas, juice and zest. Finish with the remaining bread.

BEAT THE EGGS WELL, mix with the milk and sugar, and pour this mixture over the pudding. Sprinkle with cinnamon or nutmeg and leave to soak for 30 minutes, then preheat the oven to 200°C (400°F), Gas Mark 6 and bake the pudding for 30 minutes or until set. Serve hot, on its own or with custard.

The earliest known recipe for this much-loved pudding dates from 1723. Squidgy underneath and crisp on top, the eternal question is what to serve with it: some swear by custard, others prefer cream, whilst many firmly believe that it's moist enough to need no sauce at all.

Ginger syrup pudding

SERVES 6

200g (7oz) unsalted butter, softened, plus extra for greasing

200g (7oz) soft light brown sugar

4 eggs, beaten

200g (7oz) self-raising flour

1½ tbsp ground ginger

40g (1½oz) chopped stem ginger, plus syrup from the jar

150g (5oz) golden syrup

Custard, to serve

GREASE A 1.1-LITRE (2-pint) pudding basin. In a mixing bowl, cream together the butter and sugar until pale and fluffy. Gradually add the beaten eggs to the creamed mixture, stirring after each addition — if the mixture separates, just stir in a little of the flour.

SIFT THE REMAINING FLOUR into a separate bowl together with the ground ginger, then gradually fold them into the creamed mixture, along with a small amount of syrup from the stem ginger jar. Mix well to incorporate.

POUR THE GOLDEN SYRUP into the bottom of the greased basin and add the chopped stem ginger. Spoon the sponge mixture on top. Seal the basin with a lid or foil and steam for approximately 2 hours, until the pudding is firm to the touch. Turn out onto a serving plate and serve with custard.

A pudding of contrasts, this feels as British as they come, but it's easy to forget that ginger was originally imported from Asia. The sponge has all the sweetness of childhood fare, but with a grown-up tang from the combination of stem ginger, ground ginger and ginger syrup.

Sticky toffee pudding

SERVES 4–6

100g (3½oz) chopped dates
1 tsp vanilla essence
1 tsp bicarbonate of soda
60g (2oz) unsalted butter,
   softened, plus extra
   for greasing
170g (6oz) soft light
   brown sugar
1 egg
225g (8oz) plain flour
1 tsp baking powder
Custard, to serve

For the toffee sauce
4½ tbsp double cream
15g (½oz) unsalted butter
60g (2oz) soft dark
   brown sugar

LIGHTLY GREASE A 1.1-LITRE (2-pint) pudding basin. Put the toffee sauce ingredients in a saucepan and melt together over a low heat, then pour into the greased basin and set aside.

MIX THE CHOPPED DATES, vanilla essence and bicarbonate of soda with 550ml (19fl oz) water. In a separate large bowl, cream together the butter and sugar until pale and fluffy, then gradually beat in the egg.

SIFT THE FLOUR AND BAKING POWDER together, then add to the creamed mixture in small amounts, alternating with additions of the date mixture, stirring each time to combine.

POUR THE MIXTURE over the toffee sauce in the pudding basin, cover with a lid or foil and steam for 1½ hours. Turn out and serve with custard.

Not as old as you might think, this modern classic has only been in circulation since the 1970s. Even so, its origins are lost already, with chefs in the Lake District, Lancashire, Aberdeen and the south of England all claiming to have invented it. (This in itself shows the love for sticky toffee pud up and down our nation!). It was Gary Rhodes's favourite when he visited The Pudding Club, and was recently revealed as Kate Middleton's all-time top pudding.

Syrup sponge

SERVES 4–6

200g (4oz) unsalted butter,
   softened, plus extra
   for greasing
200g (4oz) caster sugar
200g (4oz) self-raising
   flour, sifted
3 eggs, beaten with 1 tsp
   vanilla essence
3 tbsp golden syrup
Custard, to serve

GREASE A 1.1-LITRE (2-pint) pudding basin. In a mixing bowl, cream together the butter and sugar until pale and fluffy. Stir in the sifted flour a little at a time, alternating with additions of the beaten eggs and vanilla, and beating the mixture well after each addition.

PUT THE GOLDEN SYRUP in the base of the greased basin and pour the sponge mixture carefully over the top. Cover securely with a lid or foil and steam for 1½ hours. Turn out and serve with custard.

*This pudding is known to many as
treacle sponge, despite the fact that it contains
no treacle! What do you call it…?
We call it Pride of The Pudding Club!*

Rhubarb crumble

SERVES 6–8

245g (8½oz) self-raising
   flour
165g (5½oz) demerara
   sugar
60g (2oz) unsalted butter,
   cut into pieces
60g (2oz) margarine
1 tsp vanilla essence
700g (1½lb) fresh rhubarb,
   washed and cut into
   3cm (1in) pieces
2–3 tsp caster sugar
Custard or cream, to serve

SIFT THE FLOUR INTO A LARGE BOWL, add
the demerara sugar and mix well. Add the butter,
margarine and vanilla essence and mix to a fine
crumb consistency with your fingertips. Place
in the fridge to chill.

PREHEAT THE OVEN TO 200°C (400°F), Gas
Mark 6. Mix the rhubarb and caster sugar together
and place in the base of a deep, oval, ovenproof
baking dish, approx. 30 x 20cm (12 x 8in).

COVER THE RHUBARB with the chilled crumble
topping and firm down the top a little. Cook in
the oven for 35–45 minutes until golden brown.
Serve with custard or cream.

*What could be more classic and comforting than a warm
fruit crumble? Our champion version makes use of beautiful
British rhubarb. The forced variety is famously grown in the
Yorkshire triangle, a nine-square-mile area in the north
of England, where it is cultivated in dark sheds and harvested
by candlelight early in the year, whilst the flavourful
outdoor rhubarb comes into season in late spring.*

CHAMPION PUDDINGS

Summer pudding

SERVES 4–6

720g (1lb 9oz) mixed soft
  summer fruits, such as
  raspberries, strawberries,
  red- and blackcurrants
1 tbsp crème de cassis
Caster sugar, to taste
Butter, for greasing
6–8 thick slices of day-old
  white bread, crusts
  removed
Pouring or whipped cream,
  to serve

PUT THE MIXED FRUITS in a saucepan with the crème de cassis, a sprinkling of sugar and a very small amount of water. Simmer gently for 3–4 minutes to dissolve the sugar and until the fruit is soft but still holding its shape, then remove from the heat.

LIGHTLY GREASE A 1.1-LITRE (2-pint) pudding basin and completely line with most of the bread, cutting it to fit. Pour in the fruit and cover with the remaining bread to seal the pudding.

PLACE A SMALL PLATE on top of the bread and stand a heavy weight on it so that the pudding is pressed down. This will ensure the juice is absorbed, turning the bread a wonderful, rich colour. Allow to set in the fridge for a minimum of 8 hours or overnight. Turn out carefully and serve with cream.

A classic summer delight. This fruity pudding is said to have started life in Victorian spas and nursing homes, where it was served to patients as an alternative to heavy pastry or suet treats. It tastes different every time, as the combination of fruits depends on the season and the proportions used.

WHY NOT TRY...?
*Crème de mûre (blackberry liqueur) makes
a nice alternative to cassis.*

Passion fruit charlotte

SERVES 4-6

2 **Swiss rolls** (store-bought
or see page 92),
thinly sliced
12 **ripe passion fruit**
3 **gelatine leaves**
375g (13oz) **double cream**
Extra cream, to serve
(optional)

LINE A 1.1-LITRE (2-pint) pudding basin or
soufflé dish with cling film. Use the slices of Swiss
roll to line the sides and bottom of the dish.

HALVE 10 OF THE PASSION FRUIT, scrape out
the flesh into a blender and blitz to a purée. Push
through a sieve to remove the black pips.

SOAK THE GELATINE in a small bowl of cold water
until soft. Meanwhile, whip the cream in a large
bowl until it forms soft peaks. Remove the softened
gelatine from the water and carefully stir it into the
whipped cream, along with the passion fruit purée.

HALVE THE TWO REMAINING PASSION FRUIT
and scrape out the flesh into the mixture. Stir gently
until everything is incorporated. Pour the mixture
into the sponge-lined dish and leave in the fridge
to set for 2 hours or overnight. Carefully turn out
the Charlotte onto a plate and remove the cling
film. Serve on its own or with a little cream.

*This is our most popular cold pudding at The Pudding
Club. The zinginess of passion fruit cuts perfectly through
the rich cream, making this pudding a surprising delight.
Uncooked charlottes like this are related to Elizabethan
trifles, although this version is a newer twist, as passion
fruits were introduced to the UK in the 19th century.*

SCHOOL-DINNER PUDDINGS

CHAPTER 2

After the Second World War, it was made compulsory
for British schools to serve cooked meals to their pupils, and
this would normally include a pudding. Certain puds were
favoured by dinner ladies because they were low-cost and
easy to cook in large quantities for crowds of hungry
schoolchildren, and so treats such as jam roly poly, rice
pudding and treacle tart became a regular feature of school
dinner halls up and down the country. Many of the recipes
in this chapter will be remembered fondly by those who
devoured them as kids. They will fill you with warmth
and nostalgia for childhood and days gone by.

Rice pudding

SERVES 4

65g (2½oz) round
   pudding rice
1.2 litres (2 pints) creamy
   full-fat milk
25g (1oz) unsalted butter,
   cut into small pieces
50g (2oz) caster sugar
Pinch of ground nutmeg
Jam, to serve

PREHEAT THE OVEN TO 140°C (275°F), Gas Mark 1.
Put the rice into a shallow pie dish, pour over half the
milk and stir in the butter and sugar. Bake for 1 hour.

STIR IN THE REMAINING MILK and continue
to cook for another hour. Stir again, sprinkle with
nutmeg and cook for a further hour. Serve with
a spoonful of jam.

SCHOOL-DINNER PUDDINGS

Semolina pudding

SERVES 4

750ml (1 pint 6fl oz) milk
100g (3½oz) semolina
½ tsp ground cinnamon,
   plus extra for sprinkling
30g (1oz) unsalted butter,
   plus extra for greasing
100g (3½oz) caster sugar
2 egg yolks
Jam or honey, to serve
   (optional)

PREHEAT THE OVEN TO 180°C (350°F), Gas Mark 4 and thoroughly grease a shallow, ovenproof baking dish. Pour the milk into a saucepan and heat until hot but not boiling.

REMOVE THE PAN FROM THE HEAT and slowly add the semolina, whisking all the time with a balloon whisk to avoid lumps. Return the pan to the heat and bring slowly to the boil, stirring constantly so that the mixture remains smooth.

REMOVE FROM THE HEAT, stir in the cinnamon, butter, sugar and egg yolks and mix well. Pour into the greased dish and sprinkle with a little more ground cinnamon. Bake in the oven for 35–40 minutes. Serve the pudding on its own or with a generous spoonful of jam or honey.

Spotted dick

SERVES 4–6

Butter, for greasing

240g (8½oz) self-raising flour

Pinch of salt

120g (4oz) vegetable suet

30g (1oz) caster sugar

240g (8½oz) currants or raisins, soaked in brandy, then drained

Custard, to serve

GREASE A 1.1-LITRE (2-pint) pudding basin. Sift together the flour and salt into a mixing bowl, then add the suet, sugar and drained dried fruit. Mix with up to 150ml (5fl oz) cold water – enough to bring the ingredients together into a firm dough.

PUSH THE DOUGH into the greased basin and cover securely with a lid or foil. Steam the pudding for 2 hours, then turn out onto a hot plate and serve with custard.

WHY NOT TRY...?

If you want to make this pudding in the traditional shape instead of using a basin, form the mixture into a cylinder about 20cm (8in) long, and roll in a pudding cloth, before steaming for 2 hours.

We're asked about the name of this pudding more than any other. While the spots are self-explanatory, the word 'dick' is thought to derive from 'dough' or 'duff' (as still used in plum duff). It's also sometimes known as spotted dog, and has even been referred to as a blemished Richard!

SCHOOL-DINNER PUDDINGS

Bread pudding

SERVES 6–8

8 medium-thickness slices of bread (from 1 large loaf)

300ml (11fl oz) milk

300g (11oz) mixed dried fruit

50g (2oz) chopped mixed peel

1 eating apple

2 tbsp dark orange marmalade

3 tbsp soft dark brown sugar

40g (1½oz) self-raising flour

2 eggs, beaten

Squeeze of lemon juice

1 tsp ground cinnamon

100g (3½oz) unsalted butter, melted

Egg custard (see page 40) or icing sugar, to serve

PREHEAT THE OVEN TO 160°C (325°F), Gas Mark 3 and grease a 28 x 20cm (11 x 8in) roasting tin. Break up the bread, including the crusts, and soak in the milk until soft.

BEAT THE SOAKED BREAD WELL with a fork so that it becomes a soft, creamy mixture. Transfer to a large bowl and add the dried fruit and mixed peel. Grate in the unpeeled apple and stir in the marmalade, sugar, flour, eggs, lemon juice and cinnamon.

POUR HALF OF THE MELTED BUTTER into the mixture, beat well and pour into the greased tin. Pour the remaining butter in a thin stream onto the surface. Bake for 1½ hours (check regularly and cover with foil or greaseproof paper if browning too quickly). Then turn up the oven temperature to 180°C (350°F), Gas Mark 4 and bake for another 30 minutes.

SERVE HOT, cut into squares, with egg custard. Alternatively, allow to cool, then sprinkle thickly with icing sugar and slice to eat cold as a cake.

SCHOOL-DINNER PUDDINGS

Custard tart

SERVES 4–6

Butter, for greasing
225g (8oz) shortcrust
pastry (see page 10)
300ml (11fl oz) single cream
or creamy full-fat milk
2 eggs, plus 1 egg yolk
25g (1oz) caster sugar
Ground nutmeg, to sprinkle
Cream and fresh raspberries
or seasonal fruit, to serve

GREASE A LOOSE-BOTTOMED 20CM (8in) tart tin and line with the pastry (see page 11). Chill for 30 minutes in the fridge, then preheat the oven to 190°C (400°F), Gas Mark 5 and blind bake the pastry case for 25 minutes (see page 11). Remove from the oven and turn down the temperature to 170°C (325°F), Gas Mark 3.

MEANWHILE, PUT THE CREAM or milk into a saucepan and bring to the boil. Beat the eggs, egg yolk and sugar together in a bowl and then gradually whisk in the heated cream or milk.

STRAIN INTO THE COOKED PASTRY CASE and sprinkle with nutmeg. Bake in the oven for 35 minutes until the custard is set. The tart will become firmer as it becomes cold but is best eaten still slightly warm. Serve with cream and fresh raspberries or your choice of fresh fruit.

Britain has a long history of custards and creams, dating back to medieval times. They were often served alone, baked in individual cups and sometimes flavoured with fruit purées. Custard also developed into a filling for pies and tarts, as here, and eventually into the classic sauce for accompanying other desserts.

Baked custard

SERVES 4–6

Butter, for greasing
600ml (1 pint) single cream
1 vanilla pod, split in half
3 eggs
50g (2oz) caster sugar
Pinch of ground nutmeg

PREHEAT THE OVEN TO 170°C (325°F), Gas Mark 3. Lightly grease an ovenproof baking dish or straight-sided soufflé dish, 900ml–1.1 litres (1½–2 pints) capacity. Put the cream and split vanilla pod in a saucepan and heat until just at boiling point, then remove from the heat.

IN A LARGE BOWL, beat the eggs lightly with the sugar. Remove the vanilla pod from the saucepan and pour the cream onto the beaten eggs, whisking thoroughly. Strain into the greased dish and sprinkle with the nutmeg.

SIT THE BAKING DISH in a roasting tin and pour boiling water into the tin, up to the level of the mixture inside the dish. Bake in the oven for 1 hour. Serve hot or cold.

Variations

Baked coffee custard
Omit the vanilla pod and instead flavour the cream with 2 tablespoons of coffee essence or strong black coffee. Also omit the nutmeg.

Baked chocolate custard
Add 50g (2oz) chopped dark chocolate to the cream and vanilla pod before heating. Stir while heating, to ensure it melts and becomes incorporated. Omit the nutmeg.

Baked apple sponge

SERVES 4-6

200g (7oz) unsalted butter, softened, plus extra for greasing

200g (7oz) demerara sugar

3 eggs, beaten

200g (7oz) self-raising flour, sifted

2 medium cooking apples, peeled, cored and chopped

Custard or cream, to serve

PREHEAT THE OVEN TO 190°C (375°F), Gas Mark 5 and grease a 1.1-litre (2-pint) ovenproof baking dish. In a mixing bowl, cream together the butter and sugar until pale and fluffy. Gradually mix in the beaten eggs, along with a little of the flour, then fold in the remaining flour and the chopped apple.

SPOON INTO THE GREASED DISH and bake for 15 minutes, then reduce the heat to 180°C (350°F), Gas Mark 4 and continue to bake for another 20 minutes. Serve hot with custard or cream.

Eve's pudding

SERVES 4–6

450g (1lb) cooking apples, peeled, cored and chopped coarsely

75g (3oz) soft light brown sugar

100g (3½oz) unsalted butter, softened, plus extra for greasing

100g (3½oz) caster sugar, plus extra for sprinkling

2 eggs

100g (3½oz) self-raising flour, sifted

Grated zest of 1 unwaxed lemon

¼ tsp vanilla essence

Cream or custard, to serve

PREHEAT THE OVEN TO 180°C (350°F), Gas Mark 4 and grease a 1.5-litre (2½-pint) ovenproof baking dish. Put the apples into the baking dish and sprinkle with the brown sugar; mix together lightly.

IN A MIXING BOWL, cream together the butter and caster sugar until pale and fluffy, then work in the eggs, sifted flour, lemon zest and vanilla essence and mix to a soft batter. Spread this over the apples in the dish and bake for 40 minutes. Remove from the oven and sprinkle the surface with caster sugar. Serve immediately with cream or custard.

Apple and custard

SERVES 6

1kg (2lb 2oz) Bramley
apples, peeled, cored
and sliced
3 tbsp honey
Finely grated zest
of 1 unwaxed lemon

For the egg custard
600ml (1 pint) milk
6 eggs, separated
75g (3oz) caster sugar

PLACE THE APPLES, honey and lemon zest into a heavy-based saucepan and cook over a low heat until the apples are just tender. Remove from the heat and purée the apple mixture with a hand blender, then pour into a 2.3-litre (4-pint) ovenproof baking dish.

TO MAKE THE EGG CUSTARD, warm the milk in a saucepan. Beat together the egg yolks and 50g (2oz) of the sugar in a heatproof bowl, then pour in the warmed milk, stirring well. Place the bowl over a saucepan of simmering water, being careful not to let the bowl actually touch the water. Stir until the custard has thickened; this will take around 10 minutes. Pour the custard over the apple purée in the baking dish.

PREHEAT THE OVEN TO 150°C (300°F), Gas Mark 2. In a scrupulously clean bowl, whisk the egg whites until stiff, then fold in the remaining 25g (1oz) of sugar with a metal spoon. Pile the meringue over the custard, spreading it right to the edges of the dish. Bake in the oven for 30 minutes, until the meringue is golden brown.

Apple snow

SERVES 4

450g (1lb) cooking apples
    (preferably Bramley),
    peeled, cored and sliced
75g (3oz) caster sugar
Grated zest and juice
    of 1 unwaxed lemon
2 egg whites
Small, sweet biscuits,
    to serve

PUT THE SLICED APPLES, sugar, lemon zest and juice into a saucepan. Simmer over a low heat, stirring often, until the apples have become a soft, thick purée and there is no surplus liquid left in the pan. Push the apple mixture though a fine sieve or process with a hand blender until light and fluffy.

IN A SCRUPULOUSLY CLEAN BOWL, whisk the egg whites until they form soft peaks, then fold in the apple purée with a metal spoon. Spoon into glasses and chill. Serve with small, sweet biscuits.

*A favourite in Elizabethan kitchens,
cooks would often stick a sprig of rosemary
in the top of this pudding to resemble a snow–
covered tree. Bramley apples are ideal, or use
a similar variety that has a tart flavour and
becomes light and fluffy when cooked.*

SCHOOL-DINNER PUDDINGS

Queen of puddings

SERVES 4–6

180g (6½oz) breadcrumbs
Finely grated zest of
   1 unwaxed lemon
150g (5oz) caster sugar
600ml (1 pint) milk
60g (2oz) unsalted butter,
   plus extra for greasing
½ tsp vanilla essence
4 eggs, separated
100g (3½oz) strawberry
   or raspberry jam

PREHEAT THE OVEN TO 180°C (350°F), Gas Mark 4 and grease a 1.1-litre (2-pint) pie dish. Put the breadcrumbs, lemon zest and 30g (1oz) of the sugar into a mixing bowl.

COMBINE THE MILK, butter and vanilla essence in a saucepan and warm gently until the butter has melted, then pour over the breadcrumb mix. Leave the mixture to stand for 10 minutes then beat in the egg yolks. Pour the mixture into the greased pie dish and bake for 20–30 minutes until well set. Leave the oven turned on.

WARM THE JAM in a small saucepan over a low heat, then spread it generously over the pudding. In a scrupulously clean bowl, whisk the egg whites until stiff. Fold in the remaining 120g (4oz) of sugar with a metal spoon. Spread the meringue over the pudding and place back in the oven for about 10 minutes until the meringue is crisp and lightly brown.

Throughout the ages in Britain, bread was always considered a valuable commodity that should never go to waste, so this pudding started life as a way to use up precious breadcrumbs. And the name? While the 'crown' of meringue is certainly very regal, it's also said that Queen Victoria was known to enjoy a helping or two. Here at The Pudding Club, we have our very own queen of puddings — Sheila Vincent — who has been making all our sweet stuff for 16 years.

Jam roly poly

SERVES 4–6

180g (6½oz) self-raising flour, plus extra for dusting
Pinch of salt
90g (3oz) vegetable suet
Milk, to mix
450g (1lb) raspberry jam
1 tbsp caster sugar
Custard, to serve

PREHEAT THE OVEN TO 190°C (375°F), Gas Mark 5. Sift the flour and salt together into a large bowl, then add the suet and mix with enough milk to make a dough.

ON A FLOURED SURFACE, roll out the dough to about 25cm (10in) square and spread with the jam. Dampen the edges of the dough with water and roll up like a Swiss roll.

PLACE IN A ROASTING TIN and put in the oven, with one side of the tin raised so that the pudding rolls to one end. This will prevent the roly poly from unravelling. Bake for 1 hour. (Alternatively, wrap the pudding in foil to hold its shape and cover in cling film to make it watertight. Steam for 1½ hours, then carefully remove the cling film and foil.) Sprinkle the pudding with caster sugar and serve with custard.

Hugely popular in Victorian Britain, this famous pudding even features in the writing of Charles Dickens (in Bleak House*) and Beatrix Potter (in her* Tale of Samuel Whiskers*). Traditionally, the roly poly would have been boiled in a pudding cloth; but the skill of wrapping a pudding like this is now almost forgotten. At Pudding Club meetings, only spotted dick gets a bigger cheer.*

Damson cobbler

SERVES 6–8

700g (1½lb) damsons,
    halved and stoned
75g (3oz) soft light
    brown sugar
75g (3oz) unsalted butter
175g (6oz) plain flour
2 tsp baking powder
Pinch of salt
125ml (4½fl oz) milk
1 tbsp demerara sugar
Thick cream, to serve

PUT THE DAMSONS and soft brown sugar in a large saucepan and slowly bring to the boil. Cover with a lid and simmer for 3–4 minutes, then remove from the heat and allow to cool in the pan for 45–60 minutes. Pour the cooled fruit into a 23cm (9in) ovenproof baking dish, approx. 6cm (2½in) deep.

PREHEAT THE OVEN TO 220°C (425°F), Gas Mark 7. Make the cobbler topping by using your fingertips to rub the butter into the flour, baking powder and salt until they resemble fine breadcrumbs. Alternatively, do this in a food processor. Stir in the milk until you a have a sticky, dough-like mixture.

SPOON THE TOPPING over the fruit in dollops and sprinkle with the demerara sugar. Bake in the oven for 25–30 minutes, or until golden. The cobbler is best served warm with thick cream.

There are two theories on the name of this pudding. Some say it's because the finished pudding resembles street cobbles. Others believe the pudding was 'cobbled' together with whatever was to hand, by British colonists with no access to their traditional ingredients. Cobblers were promoted by the British Ministry of Food during the Second World War, since they are hearty and filling, but could be made with margarine instead of heavily rationed butter.

SCHOOL-DINNER PUDDINGS

Jam and coconut sponge

SERVES 4–6

3 tbsp blackcurrant jam
200g (7oz) unsalted butter,
    softened, plus extra
    for greasing
200g (7oz) caster sugar
200g (7oz) self-raising
    flour, sifted
60g (2oz) desiccated
    coconut
3 eggs, beaten
Custard, to serve

GREASE A 1.1-LITRE (2-pint) pudding basin. Put the jam in the bottom of the basin. In a mixing bowl, cream together the butter and sugar until pale and fluffy.

ADD THE SIFTED FLOUR to the creamed mixture a little at a time, along with gradual additions of the desiccated coconut and beaten egg, mixing well each time. Pour the sponge mixture carefully over the jam in the basin. Cover securely with a lid or foil and steam for 1½–2 hours. Turn out and serve with custard.

Any red-fruit jam is good, but use the best-quality you can find — home-made is best.

Banana fritters

SERVES 6

200g (7oz) self-raising flour

1 tbsp baking powder

30g (1oz) golden caster sugar, plus extra for dusting

1 egg, beaten

300ml (11fl oz) milk

Grated zest of 1 unwaxed lemon

½ tsp ground nutmeg

6 bananas

Vegetable or sunflower oil, for deep-frying

Ice cream, to serve

TO PREPARE THE BATTER, combine the flour, baking powder and sugar in a mixing bowl. Gradually add the egg and milk and whisk to form a smooth batter. Set aside to rest for up to 1 hour, then mix the lemon zest and nutmeg into the rested batter.

PEEL THE BANANAS and cut them in half. In a deep, heavy-based saucepan, heat enough oil to submerge the banana halves. To check the oil is at the right temperature, drop in a small piece of bread to see whether it sizzles and browns. When the oil is hot enough, dip the banana pieces into the batter and deep-fry until golden. Remove with a slotted spoon and drain briefly on kitchen paper. Dust the fritters with a little caster sugar and serve with ice cream.

Manchester tart

SERVES 4–6

225g (8oz) shortcrust pastry (see page 10), chilled
3 tbsp good-quality raspberry jam
3 tbsp desiccated or flaked coconut
2 tbsp custard powder
2 tbsp caster sugar
600ml (1 pint) milk
Cream, to serve

ROLL OUT THE CHILLED PASTRY on a floured surface until 5mm (¼in) thick, then use it to line a 20cm (8in) tart dish (see page 11). Refrigerate the lined dish for 30 minutes, then preheat the oven to 190°C (400°F), Gas Mark 5 and blind bake for 25 minutes (see page 11). Remove from the oven and set to aside to cool.

WHEN COOL, spread the pastry case with the jam and sprinkle with half the coconut. In a medium bowl, mix the custard powder and sugar with a little cold milk to form a paste. Heat the remaining milk gently in a saucepan, pour onto the custard paste and whisk to combine, then return the mixture to the saucepan and bring to the boil to thicken.

POUR THE CUSTARD over the jam in the pastry case, sprinkle with the remaining coconut and leave to set in the fridge. Serve cold, with a little cream.

Many will remember this pudding fondly, as a feature of school-dinner menus from the 1950s onwards. With its pastry base, hidden layer of jam, creamy custard and generous coconut topping, it's considered a simpler, more modern variation on the traditional Manchester pudding (see page 108).

Pineapple upside-down pudding

SERVES 4–6

2 heaped tbsp golden syrup

1 x 400g tin of pineapple
   rings, drained

4 glacé cherries, halved

120g (4oz) caster sugar

120g (4oz) unsalted butter,
   softened, plus extra for
   greasing

2 large eggs, beaten

120g (4oz) self-raising
   flour, sifted

1 tsp baking powder

Cream, ice cream or
   custard, to serve

PREHEAT THE OVEN TO 170°C (325°F), Gas Mark 3. Grease a 20cm (8in) sandwich tin and line the base with non-stick baking parchment. Spread the golden syrup across the base of the tin and arrange the pineapple rings and cherries on top.

PLACE THE SUGAR, BUTTER, EGGS, flour and baking powder in a mixing bowl and beat together with an electric hand mixer until smooth and pale in colour. Spread the mixture evenly over the pineapple rings in the tin.

BAKE IN THE OVEN FOR 50–60 minutes until the sponge is golden and just shrinking away from the sides of the tin. Invert onto a plate and serve hot or cold, with cream, ice cream or custard.

Treacle tart

225g (8oz) shortcrust
  pastry (see page 10),
  chilled
180ml (6fl oz) golden syrup
60g (2oz) breadcrumbs
Finely grated zest and juice
  of 1 unwaxed lemon
  or orange
1 egg, beaten
Vanilla ice cream, to serve

PREHEAT THE OVEN TO 190°C (375°F), Gas Mark 5. Roll out three quarters of the pastry on the floured surface and use it to line a 20cm (8in) pie dish (see page 11). Reserve the rest of the pastry to use for decoration.

WARM THE GOLDEN SYRUP gently in a saucepan or the microwave, mix with the breadcrumbs and spread in the uncooked pastry case. Pour over the lemon or orange juice and sprinkle with the zest.

ROLL OUT THE REMAINING PASTRY and cut into strips 1cm (½in) wide. Arrange them over the filling in a criss-cross pattern to make a pretty lattice top. Brush with beaten egg and bake in the oven for 30–40 minutes. Serve with vanilla ice cream.

FAMILY FAVOURITES

Everyone enjoys something sweet at the end of a meal and this chapter is full of satisfying puddings that are bound to please the whole family. Whether you want a quick midweek pudding or an easy weekend treat, these simple but delicious options are ideal for when time and ingredients are limited. Our toffee apple pudding will be a big hit with the kids, Bakewell tart is bound to impress Granny or any unexpected guests, and lemon meringue pie will have everyone clamouring for second helpings. Many of these much-loved staple recipes were passed down the generations of our own families and have stood the test of time, so we hope that some of them may become a regular part of your repertoire.

Sticky pear pudding

SERVES 4–6

2 large pears
Juice of 1 lemon
150g (5oz) unsalted butter,
  plus extra for greasing
90g (3oz) demerara sugar
2 tbsp golden syrup
120g (4oz) caster sugar
2 eggs, beaten
150g (5oz) self-raising flour
2 tbsp milk
Custard, to serve

GREASE A 1.1-LITRE (2-pint) pudding basin. Peel the pears, remove the cores and cut lengthways into slices of 1cm (½in) thickness. Place in a saucepan with the lemon juice and a little boiling water and poach over a gentle heat for 3 minutes.

PUT 30g (1oz) of the butter in a saucepan with the demerara sugar and golden syrup and cook gently until the butter has melted and the sugar has dissolved. Pour this caramel mixture over the bottom and sides of the greased basin. Arrange the pear slices over the sides and base, pressing them firmly into the caramel.

IN A MIXING BOWL, beat the remaining butter with the caster sugar until pale and fluffy. Gradually beat in the eggs, then stir in the flour and milk. Spoon the mixture over the pears in the basin and level the surface. Bake for about 1 hour or until firm to the touch and golden brown. Turn out carefully and serve with custard.

Strawberry jam omelette

SERVES 4

1 tbsp caster sugar
2 tbsp double or
  whipping cream
4 eggs, separated
30g (1oz) unsalted butter
45g (1½oz) good-quality
  strawberry jam
2 tbsp icing sugar
Cream or custard, to serve

IN A LARGE BOWL, beat the caster sugar, cream and egg yolks until pale. In a separate bowl, beat the egg whites until they form soft peaks. Gently fold this into the yolk mix.

PREHEAT THE GRILL TO A MEDIUM HEAT. Melt the butter in a medium, ovenproof frying pan until it starts to foam, then add the egg mix. Cook over a low heat for 1–2 minutes until the base of the omelette is set. Place under the grill for 2–3 minutes until the top has just set.

MEANWHILE, WARM THE JAM in a small saucepan or the microwave. Spread this on top of the cooked omelette and sprinkle with the icing sugar. Fold the omelette in half and serve with cream or custard.

Spicy apple layer pudding

SERVES 4–6

Butter, for greasing
2 tbsp golden syrup
150g (5oz) demerara sugar
120g (4oz) sultanas
2 tbsp lemon juice
4 large cooking apples,
    cored peeled and sliced
1 tsp ground cinnamon
Custard, to serve

For the suet pastry
225g (8oz) self-raising
    flour, plus extra for
    dusting
Pinch of salt
120g (4oz) vegetable suet

TO MAKE THE SUET PASTRY, sift the flour and salt into a mixing bowl, add the suet and mix with 150ml (5fl oz) cold water to form a stiff dough. Divide roughly into four pieces, place on a floured surface and press or roll out into circles, graduating in size to fit a 1.1-litre (2-pint) pudding basin.

GREASE THE BASIN. Spoon the golden syrup into the bottom of the basin. Mix the remaining ingredients together. Place the smallest circle of pastry in the basin, then add a layer of the apple filling, then alternate with pastry and filling, finishing with the largest circle of pastry on top. Cover securely with a lid or foil and steam for 2½ hours. Turn out onto a serving dish and serve with custard.

SERVES 4-6

90g (3oz) unsalted butter, plus extra for greasing

240g (8½oz) self-raising flour, sifted

90g (3oz) caster sugar

Finely grated zest of ½ unwaxed lemon (juice to serve)

½ tsp ground cinnamon

1 egg, beaten

Milk, to mix

3 tbsp golden syrup, plus optional extra to serve

1 large cooking apple, peeled and cored

Custard, to serve

GREASE A 1.7-LITRE (3-pint) pudding basin. Put the butter and sifted flour in a mixing bowl and, using your fingertips, rub together until the texture is like fine crumbs, then stir in the sugar, lemon zest and cinnamon. Mix in the egg and enough milk to reach a soft dropping consistency.

POUR THE GOLDEN SYRUP into the bottom of the greased basin. Thinly slice the apple and arrange the slices fanned out in a circle on top of the syrup. Spoon in the sponge mixture, cover securely with a lid or foil and steam for 1½ hours. Turn out and serve with custard, or golden syrup melted with a little lemon juice.

Apple brown Betty

SERVES 6

800g (1¾lb) peeled,
   chopped Bramley apple
½ tsp ground cinnamon
Grated zest and juice
   of 2 oranges
25g (1oz) demerara sugar
200g (7oz) sweet biscuits
   (digestives or similar),
   crushed
50g (2oz) breadcrumbs
50g (2oz) flaked or
   chopped nuts
50g (2oz) unsalted butter
Cream or ice cream, to serve

PREHEAT THE OVEN TO 175°C (340°F), Gas Mark 3–4. Mix together the chopped apple, cinnamon, orange juice and half the zest in a shallow, 20cm (8in) square, ovenproof baking dish.

COMBINE THE SUGAR, crushed biscuits, breadcrumbs and nuts with the rest of the orange zest and spread this over the apple mixture. Place small pieces of butter across the top of the crumb mix.

BAKE IN THE OVEN FOR 30–40 minutes until the apple is cooked and the crumb top is crisp and brown. Serve with cream or ice cream.

This family recipe comes from Jill Coombe, from The Pudding Club. She inherited it from Granny Coombe, who baked it regularly. It's quick to make and a bit of cheat, but absolutely delicious nonetheless.

Baked apples

SERVES 4

4 cooking apples, such as Bramley Seedling

75g (3oz) unsalted butter, plus extra for greasing

Pinch of ground ginger or cinnamon

100g (3½oz) soft light brown sugar

Chilled thick cream or ice cream, to serve

PREHEAT THE OVEN TO 180°C (350°F), Gas Mark 4. Wipe and core the apples. Make a shallow cut round the middle circumference of the apples, piercing the skin but going no deeper, so that the apples don't burst during cooking.

GREASE A SHALLOW, ovenproof baking dish that can hold all the apples tightly. Place the apples in the dish and put a piece of butter into the cavity of each, followed by a pinch of your chosen spice, then fill up each apple with sugar. Dot the top of the apples with the remaining butter. If you have any sugar or butter remaining, distribute it across the bottom of the dish.

BAKE THE APPLES FOR 30 minutes or until their centres are soft and fluffy and the butter and sugar have turned into a thin toffee. Serve straight from the oven with chilled thick cream or ice cream.

If you find yourself in Kent visit the National Fruit Collection at Brogdale Farm near Faversham. There are a huge number of apple and other fruit trees and cultivars.

Baked apples in blankets

SERVES 4

Butter, for greasing
Plain flour, for dusting
300g (11oz) shortcrust
 pastry (see page 10)
½ tsp mixed spice
50g (2oz) caster sugar
50g (2oz) sultanas
1 tbsp brandy
4 medium Bramley apples
1 egg, beaten
Milk, for brushing
Custard, to serve

PREHEAT THE OVEN TO 200°C (400°F), Gas Mark 6 and grease a baking sheet. On a floured surface, roll out the pastry and cut into four squares, each large enough to fully encase a whole apple.

COMBINE THE MIXED SPICE, sugar, sultanas and brandy together in a small bowl. Peel and core the apples and place one in the centre of each pastry square. Fill the hole in each apple with the spice mixture. Pull up the edges of the pastry so that the apples are enclosed and press together at the top.

ARRANGE THE PASTRY PARCELS on the greased baking sheet with the joins positioned underneath. Brush with beaten egg and milk and bake in the oven for 30 minutes until golden brown. Serve with custard.

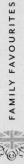

Apple tart

SERVES 6–8

900g (2lb) Bramley or Cox apples, peeled and cored
100g (3½oz) caster sugar
2 tbsp lemon juice
225g (8 oz) shortcrust pastry (see page 10), chilled
100g (3½oz) apricot jam
Cream or ice cream, to serve

SLICE 700g (1½lb) OF THE PEELED, cored apples and place in a saucepan with the sugar, lemon juice and 100ml (3½fl oz) water. Bring to the boil and simmer until the apple breaks down into a pulp. Pass through a sieve and leave to cool.

ROLL OUT THE CHILLED PASTRY on a floured surface until 5mm (¼in) thick and use it to line a 23cm (9in) tart dish (see page 11). Refrigerate for 30 minutes, then preheat the oven to 190°C (400°F), Gas Mark 5 and blind bake the pastry case for 25 minutes (see page 11). Remove from the oven and set aside. Leave the oven turned on.

PLACE THE COOLED APPLE PURÉE in the cooked pastry case and smooth the surface. Slice the remaining apple thinly and place neatly onto the tart in a circle, gradually overlapping the slices until the apple purée is completely covered.

RETURN THE TART TO THE OVEN and bake for 20–25 minutes. As soon as you've removed the tart from the oven, heat the apricot jam in a small saucepan or the microwave. Use a pastry brush to brush the melted jam onto the apple to give it a nice glaze. Serve the tart warm or cold, with cream or ice cream.

Apple flapjack

SERVES 4–6

960g (2lb 2oz) cooking apples, peeled, cored and sliced
6 tbsp caster sugar
4 tbsp golden syrup
170g (6oz) unsalted butter, plus extra for greasing
240g (8½oz) rolled oats
¼ tsp salt
1 tsp ground ginger
Icing sugar, to dredge
Custard, to serve

PLACE MOST OF THE APPLE SLICES in a saucepan (reserve a few slices for decoration) with 3½ tablespoons of the caster sugar, cover with a lid and simmer gently until soft and pulpy.

PUT 2 TABLESPOONS OF CASTER SUGAR in another saucepan with the golden syrup and 150g (5oz) of the butter, and heat gently until dissolved. Remove from the heat and stir in the oats, salt and ginger.

PREHEAT THE OVEN TO 190°C (375°F), Gas Mark 5 and grease a shallow 20cm (8in) pie dish. Use three-quarters of the oat mixture to line the base and sides up to 2.5cm (1in) from the top. Pour over the apple mixture and cover with the remaining oat mixture. Press down lightly.

BAKE IN THE OVEN FOR ABOUT 35 minutes. Just before the end of the cooking time, gently fry the reserved apple slices in the remaining butter and about 1 teaspoon of caster sugar. Remove the flapjack from the oven and dredge with icing sugar. Decorate with the fried apple slices and serve with custard.

FAMILY FAVOURITES

Toffee apple pudding

SERVES 6

200g (7oz) unsalted butter, softened, plus extra for greasing
200g (7oz) soft light brown sugar
4 eggs, beaten
200g (7oz) self-raising flour, sifted
150g (5oz) peeled, cored and chopped Bramley apple
Custard, to serve

For the toffee sauce
30g (1oz) unsalted butter
70ml (2½fl oz) whipping cream
85g (3oz) soft dark brown sugar

GREASE A 1.1-LITRE (2-pint) pudding basin. In a mixing bowl, cream together the butter and sugar until pale and fluffy. Add the beaten eggs a small amount at a time — if the mixture separates, just stir in a little of the flour. Gradually fold in the remaining flour, then add 100g (3½oz) of the chopped apple and mix well.

TO MAKE THE TOFFEE SAUCE, put the butter, cream and dark brown sugar in a saucepan, bring to the boil and simmer until the sauce thickens slightly. Pour the sauce into the bottom of the greased basin, add the remaining 50g (2oz) of chopped apple, then pour the sponge mixture on top.

SEAL THE BASIN with a lid or foil and steam for approximately 2 hours until firm to the touch. Turn out onto a serving plate and serve with custard.

For the English, toffee apples are synonymous with Bonfire Night, but in Scotland, Ireland and the US, these sugary treats-on sticks are more commonly eaten at Halloween.

WHY NOT TRY...?
It's nice to serve a little extra toffee sauce alongside this. Simply increase the sauce quantities as you wish, and keep back the extra proportion when filling the basin.

FAMILY FAVOURITES

Apple charlotte

SERVES 4

450g (1lb) peeled, cored
and chopped apples
(Bramley or Cox are ideal)
1 tbsp caster sugar
110g (4oz) unsalted butter
6 medium-thickness slices of
bread, crusts removed
1 egg yolk
Cream or custard, to serve

PLACE THE CHOPPED APPLES in a saucepan with the sugar and 25g (1oz) of the butter. Cook over a low heat until soft and broken down. Remove from the heat and purée the apple in the pan with a hand blender. Leave to cool.

MELT THE REMAINING 85g (3oz) of butter in a saucepan or the microwave and brush it over one side of each bread slice, making sure the bread is well covered. Cut into rectangles and use most of them to line a 20–25cm (8–10in) pudding basin or round cake tin, 12cm (4½in) in depth, placing the pieces buttered-side down and slightly overlapping (reserve a little bread for the top). Press down firmly.

PREHEAT THE OVEN TO 180°C (350°F), Gas Mark 4. When the apple purée is cool, whisk in the egg yolk and pour the mixture into the bread-lined basin or tin. Cover with the remaining sliced bread, butter-side up, and press down firmly. Bake in the oven for 45 minutes, until golden brown. Carefully turn out onto a warmed plate and serve with cream or custard.

Blackberry, apple and cinnamon crumble

SERVES 6-8

245g (8½oz) self-raising flour

½ tsp ground cinnamon

165g (5½oz) demerara sugar

60g (2oz) unsalted butter, cut into pieces

60g (2oz) margarine

1 tsp vanilla essence

450g (1lb) peeled, cored and sliced Bramley apples

250g (9oz) blackberries

Caster sugar, to taste

Custard or cream, to serve

TO PREPARE THE CRUMBLE TOPPING, sift the flour and cinnamon together into a mixing bowl, add the demerara sugar and mix well. Add the butter, margarine and vanilla essence and mix to a fine crumb consistency with your fingertips. Place in the fridge to chill.

PREHEAT THE OVEN TO 200°C (400°F), Gas Mark 6. Mix the apples and blackberries together with caster sugar to taste and place in the bottom of a deep, 30cm (12in) oval ovenproof baking dish.

ADD THE CRUMBLE TOPPING and press to firm the top a little. Bake in the oven for 35–45 minutes until golden brown. Serve with custard or cream.

You can substitute part of the self-raising flour with porridge oats. You can also use chopped hazelnuts for added crunch.

FAMILY FAVOURITES

Cinnamon and apple bread pudding

SERVES 6

Butter, for greasing

300g (11oz) white bread, cut into approx. 1cm (½in) cubes

300g (11oz) peeled, cored and chopped cooking apple

120g (4oz) golden caster sugar

2 tsp ground cinnamon

200ml (7fl oz) milk

200ml (7fl oz) whipping cream

4 eggs

2 tsp vanilla essence

Toffee sauce, to serve (see page 64)

PREHEAT THE OVEN TO 180°C (350°F), Gas Mark 4 and grease a 30cm (12in) oval ovenproof baking dish. Place about half the bread cubes and chopped apple in the bottom, making sure they are evenly mixed in the dish.

MIX TOGETHER THE SUGAR and cinnamon in a small bowl. Sprinkle about half over the bread and apple, then spread the remaining bread and apple on top. Whisk together the milk, cream, eggs and vanilla essence until well combined. Pour this over the pudding and leave for 10–15 minutes for the liquid to be absorbed into the bread.

SPRINKLE THE REMAINING SUGAR and cinnamon onto the top and bake in the oven for 35–45 minutes until golden brown. The centre of the pudding should still be nice and moist and the top crispy. Serve with toffee sauce.

Lemon sponge

SERVES 4–6

200g (7oz) unsalted butter, softened, plus extra for greasing

200g (7oz) caster sugar

3 eggs, beaten

200g (7oz) self-raising flour, sifted

Finely grated zest and juice of 1 unwaxed lemon

3 tbsp lemon curd

Custard, to serve

GREASE A 1.1-LITRE (2-pint) pudding basin. In a mixing bowl, cream together the butter and sugar until pale and fluffy. Gradually add the beaten egg — if the mixture separates, just stir in a little of the flour. Fold in the remaining flour and the lemon zest and juice.

PUT THE LEMON CURD in the base of the greased basin and pour the sponge mixture carefully over the top. Cover securely with a lid or foil and steam for 1½ hours. Turn out and serve with custard.

Variation

Lemon and syrup sponge
Make as described, but using golden caster sugar and omitting the lemon juice from the sponge mixture. Instead of lemon curd, warm 3 tablespoons of golden syrup in a saucepan or the microwave, mix with the lemon juice and place in the basin. Pour the sponge mixture over the top, cover and steam for 2 hours. Serve with extra syrup mixed with lemon juice, as well as custard or ice cream.

FAMILY FAVOURITES

Lemon meringue pie

SERVES 6

Flour, for dusting
225g (8oz) shortcrust
   pastry (see page 10)
3 tbsp cornflour
225g (8oz) caster sugar
Grated zest and juice of
   2 large, unwaxed lemons
3 large eggs, separated
40g (1½oz) unsalted butter
Pouring cream, to serve

ON A FLOURED SURFACE, roll out the pastry to a circle 2cm (¾in) larger in diameter than the rim of a deep 20cm (8in) pie dish. Cut a 1cm (½in) strip from all the way around the edge of the pastry, dampen the rim of the dish and press on the strip. Line the dish with the pastry circle (see page 11), ensuring no air is trapped underneath. Prick the base all over with a fork and put in the fridge for 30 minutes; this helps to prevent the pastry shrinking while baking.

PREHEAT THE OVEN TO 190°C (375°F), Gas Mark 5 and blind bake the chilled pastry case for 25 minutes or until cooked through (see page 11). Remove from the oven and turn down the temperature to 150°C (300°F), Gas Mark 2.

MEANWHILE, MAKE THE FILLING. Measure 275ml (½ pint) cold water into a jug and spoon the cornflour and 50g (2oz) of the sugar into a bowl. Add enough of the water to mix to a smooth paste, then pour the remaining water into a small saucepan and add the lemon zest. Bring to the boil and then pour this gradually onto the cornflour paste, mixing all the time until smooth.

RETURN THE MIXTURE TO THE PAN and bring back to the boil, still mixing continuously. Simmer very gently for about 1 minute, continuing to stir. Remove the pan from the heat and beat in the egg yolks, lemon juice and butter. Pour the lemon mixture into the pastry case and spread out evenly.

(continued overleaf)

(continued from previous page)

TO MAKE THE MERINGUE, whisk the egg whites in a large, scrupulously clean bowl until they form stiff peaks. Whisk in the remaining 175g (6oz) of sugar about a quarter at a time, until completely incorporated. With a palette knife, spread the meringue over the lemon filling in the pastry case, taking it right to the edges of the pastry rim so that the pie is sealed. If you wish, you can make decorative swirls in the meringue using the palette knife.

BAKE ON THE CENTRE SHELF of the oven for 45 minutes, by which time the meringue will be pale beige, crisp on the outside and soft within. Serve warm or cold (but leave to settle for 20 minutes if serving warm). Accompany with chilled pouring cream.

It is widely believed that meringue was invented in the Swiss town of Meiringen in 1720, although doubts have been raised by a similar recipe discovered in an earlier French cookbook, and by the appearance of the word 'meringue' in an earlier edition of the English dictionary. But whatever the truth — Swiss or French — nobody can argue that the lemon meringue pie has developed a truly British identity.

Banoffee pudding

SERVES 4–6

3 ripe bananas

120g (4oz) unsalted butter, softened, plus extra for greasing

120g (4oz) caster sugar

1 large egg

1 tbsp milk

120g (4oz) self-raising flour

½ tsp baking powder

2 tsp lemon juice

Custard, to serve

For the toffee sauce

4½ tbsp double cream

15g (½oz) unsalted butter

60g (2oz) soft dark brown sugar

LIGHTLY GREASE A 1.1-LITRE (2-pint) pudding basin. Place the sauce ingredients in a saucepan and melt together over a low heat. Peel and slice one banana and put in the bottom of the greased basin. Pour in the toffee sauce.

IN A MIXING BOWL, cream together the butter and sugar, then beat in the egg and milk. Sift the flour and baking powder together into a separate bowl. Peel the remaining two bananas and mash with the lemon juice. Stir the mashed bananas into the creamed mixture then fold in the sifted flour.

MIX TO ENSURE EVERYTHING is well incorporated and pour into the basin. Cover well with a lid or foil and steam for 1½ hours. Turn out onto a plate and serve with custard.

The combination of bananas and toffee was devised by a Sussex chef in the early 1970s, as the well-known pie of the same name. It proved instantly popular in Britain and quickly caught on around the world. In this recipe the flavours have been translated into a delicious sponge pudding.

FAMILY FAVOURITES

Orange upside-down pudding

SERVES 6–8

125g (4½oz) unsalted butter, softened, plus extra for greasing

125g (4½oz) caster sugar

2 eggs

125g (4½oz) self-raising flour

2 sweet oranges

4 tbsp golden syrup

2 balls of stem ginger

Whipped cream or ice cream, to serve

PREHEAT THE OVEN TO 180°C (350°F), Gas Mark 4 and grease a deep 20cm (8in) cake tin. In a mixing bowl, cream together the butter and sugar until pale and fluffy. Add the eggs one at a time – if the mixture starts to split, just add a little of the flour. Zest one of the oranges and add the grated zest to the creamed mixture, then fold in the remaining flour.

SPOON THE GOLDEN SYRUP into the bottom of the greased tin and spread to cover the base. Peel both oranges, removing the skin and pith. Slice them thinly and arrange the slices overlapping on top of the golden syrup. Slice the stem ginger and place on top of the orange slices.

SPREAD THE SPONGE MIXTURE over the orange and ginger slices. Bake in the oven for 35–40 minutes until firm. Leave to cool, then turn out onto a serving plate and serve with whipped cream or ice cream.

FAMILY FAVOURITES

Seville orange marmalade puddings

MAKES 8

- 240g (8½oz) good-quality, thick-cut, Seville orange marmalade
- 200g (7oz) unsalted butter, softened, plus extra for greasing
- 200g (7oz) caster sugar
- 4 eggs
- ½ tsp vanilla essence
- 200g (7oz) self-raising flour, sifted
- Grated zest and juice of 1 orange
- Custard, to serve

GREASE EIGHT 150–200ml (5–7fl oz) ovenproof pudding basins. Place 30g (1oz) of the marmalade into the bottom of each.

IN A MIXING BOWL, cream together the butter and sugar until pale and fluffy. Add the eggs and vanilla essence – if the mixture separates, just stir in a little of the sifted flour. Fold the remaining flour into the creamed mixture and stir well. Finally add the orange zest and juice.

DIVIDE THE MIXTURE EVENLY between the pudding basins. Seal with lids or foil and steam for 45–60 minutes until cooked. Turn out and serve with custard.

Seville oranges are only available for a very short time at the beginning of the year, so look out for them if you want to make your own marmalade.

Rhubarb and ginger puddings

MAKES 8

200g (7oz) fresh rhubarb

50g (2oz) stem ginger, finely chopped

200ml (7fl oz) ginger syrup (from the stem ginger jar)

200g (7oz) unsalted butter, softened, plus extra for greasing

200g (7oz) caster sugar

4 eggs

200g (7oz) self-raising flour

½ tsp baking powder

2 tbsp ground ginger

Grated zest and juice of 1 orange

Custard, vanilla ice cream or vanilla yoghurt, to serve

GREASE EIGHT 200ml (7fl oz) pudding basins. Chop the rhubarb into 2–3cm (¾–1in) pieces. Drain the stem ginger and measure out the required syrup from the jar. Put 5 teaspoons of the ginger syrup into each basin and top with 25g (1oz) of the chopped rhubarb.

IN A MIXING BOWL, cream together the butter and sugar until pale and fluffy. Gradually add the eggs — if the mixture separates, just stir in a little of the flour. Sift the remaining flour into a separate bowl, together with the baking powder and ground ginger. Fold them into the creamed mixture and stir well to incorporate.

ADD THE ORANGE ZEST and juice and the chopped stem ginger. The mixture should be fairly fluid; divide it evenly between the greased basins and seal with lids or foil. Steam for 45–60 minutes. Turn out and serve with custard, vanilla ice cream or vanilla yoghurt.

Plum and almond puddings

MAKES 8

100g (3½oz) unsalted butter, softened

100g (3½oz) caster sugar

2 eggs

½ tsp almond essence

100g (3½oz) self-raising flour

50g (2oz) ground almonds

240g (8½oz) diced or sliced Victoria plums

40g (1½oz) golden syrup

Thick cream or vanilla ice cream, to serve

PREHEAT THE OVEN TO 180°C (350°F), Gas Mark 4. In a mixing bowl, cream together the butter and sugar until pale and fluffy. Add the eggs and almond essence — if the mixture separates, just stir in a little of the flour. Fold in the remaining flour and ground almonds and mix well.

PLACE 30g (1oz) of the plums and about 1 teaspoon of the syrup in the bottom of eight 200ml (7fl oz) ovenproof pudding basins. Pour 80g (3oz) of the sponge mix into each basin and bake for approximately 15 minutes, until firm to the touch and golden brown. Turn out and serve with thick cream or vanilla ice cream.

The Pudding Club is on the edge of the Vale of Evesham — one of the fruit-growing centres of England — and we created this recipe when we had a glut of plums one year. The best plums are Victoria, delicious to eat on their own, or spoil yourself and use a few in this recipe.

Bakewell tart

SERVES 8

375g (13oz) shortcrust
   pastry (see page 10),
   chilled
225g (8oz) unsalted butter,
   softened
225g (8oz) caster sugar
225g (8oz) ground almonds
3 eggs
50g (2oz) plain flour,
   plus extra for dusting
Grated zest of 1 unwaxed
   lemon
350g (12oz) good-quality
   raspberry jam
25g (1oz) flaked almonds
Custard or cream, to serve

ROLL OUT THE CHILLED PASTRY on a floured surface until 5mm (¼in) thick and use it to line a 30cm (12in) tart dish (see page 11). Refrigerate for 30 minutes, then preheat the oven to 190°C (400°F), Gas Mark 5 and blind bake the chilled pastry case for 25 minutes (see page 11). Remove from the oven and set aside. Reduce the oven temperature to 180°C (350°F), Gas Mark 4.

TO MAKE THE FILLING, cream together the butter and sugar in a mixing bowl until pale and fluffy. Mix in the ground almonds, then add the eggs to the mixture one at a time, mixing well with each addition. If the mixture separates, just stir in a little of the flour. Finally, add the remaining flour and lemon zest and mix to combine.

SPREAD THE RASPBERRY JAM across the base of the cooked pastry case. Pour the filling over the jam and level it out. Sprinkle the flaked almonds on top. Bake in the oven for 20 minutes, until set and golden brown. Allow to cool and serve with custard or cream.

Many think this is the original confection from the Derbyshire town, but they are sadly mistaken, as this tart is the pretender to the Bakewell pudding throne (see page 103). It has become famous nonetheless, along with the much-disputed theory that it came about when a recipe for jam tarts went wrong.

FORGOTTEN PUDDINGS

CHAPTER 4

Some British puddings can be traced back as far as
the 15th century. With such a long-tailed history, it's no
surprise that we have so many to choose from. But over
the years, trends for sweet treats have come and gone,
and many once-loved puds are now almost forgotten.
So in this chapter we want to remind everyone about some
neglected puddings that deserve to be cooked and enjoyed
anew! Many of them will be unknown to you; we hope
you will give them a try and enjoy learning the quirky stories
about their origins and how they gained their names.
We'd love you to share these puddings with your
friends and help us save them from extinction.

Duchess's pudding

SERVES 4–6

120g (4oz) unsalted butter, softened, plus extra for greasing

120g (4oz) caster sugar

2 eggs, beaten

150g (5oz) self-raising flour

60g (2oz) mixed dried fruit

30g (1oz) glacé cherries, chopped

30g (1oz) shelled walnuts, chopped

Few drops of almond essence

Milk, to mix

Custard, to serve

GREASE A 1.1-LITRE (2-pint) pudding basin. In a mixing bowl, cream together the butter and sugar until pale and fluffy. Gradually add the eggs to the creamed mixture, beating well after each addition.

SIFT IN THE FLOUR, then add the mixed fruit, cherries, nuts, almond essence and enough milk to give a soft dropping consistency. Pour into the greased basin, cover with a lid or foil and steam for 1½–2 hours. Turn out and serve with custard.

Duke of Cambridge tart

SERVES 6

225g (8oz) shortcrust
pastry (see page 10)
Plain flour, for dusting
50g (2oz) chopped mixed
candied peel
50g (2oz) glacé cherries,
chopped
25g (1oz) angelica, chopped
75g (3oz) unsalted butter
75g (3oz) caster sugar
2 egg yolks
Cream, to serve

GREASE AN 18cm (7in) tart or sandwich tin.
Alternatively, you can use six individual tart tins.
Roll out the pastry on a floured surface and use it
to line the greased tin(s). Chill in the fridge for 30
minutes to avoid the pastry shrinking while baking.

PREHEAT THE OVEN TO 190°C (375°F), Gas
Mark 5. Sprinkle the chilled pastry with the chopped
candied peel, cherries and angelica. Put the butter,
sugar and egg yolks into a small saucepan and bring
to the boil, beating with a wooden spoon. When
boiling, pour over the fruit in the pastry case(s).

BAKE IN THE OVEN FOR 30–40 MINUTES; check
after 30 minutes and cover with foil if the pastry is
browning too much. Individual tarts will need less
cooking time (give them 20–25 minutes but check
them regularly). Serve warm with cream.

Oxford pudding

SERVES 4–6

Butter, for greasing
60g (2oz) soft dark
    brown sugar
180g (6½oz) self-raising
    flour
Pinch of salt
60g (2oz) ground rice
120g (4oz) shredded suet
120g (4oz) golden syrup,
    plus extra to serve
120g (4oz) thick-cut
    marmalade
1 egg, beaten
2 tbsp milk
Custard, to serve

THOROUGHLY GREASE A 1.1-LITRE (2-pint) pudding basin and press the sugar onto the sides and the base. Sift the flour and salt together into a mixing bowl and add the ground rice. Stir in the suet, golden syrup and marmalade.

MIX TOGETHER THE BEATEN EGG AND MILK, then pour this onto the other ingredients, mixing well to combine. Pour into the greased basin, cover with a lid or foil and steam for 3 hours, topping up with boiling water as necessary. Turn out and serve with warmed golden syrup and custard.

Poor knights of Windsor

SERVES 4-6

3 tbsp single cream

2 eggs

3 tbsp medium sherry

1 tbsp ground cinnamon

2 tbsp caster sugar

6 slices of day-old white
  bread, 1.25cm (½in)
  thick, crusts removed

Unsalted butter, for frying

Jam, to serve

BEAT THE CREAM, EGGS AND SHERRY together well. Mix the cinnamon and sugar together in a small bowl. Cut each slice of bread into three wide fingers and dip each piece into the egg mixture to coat both sides.

MELT THE BUTTER IN A LARGE FRYING PAN until sizzling. Fry the coated bread slices until crisp and golden brown on both sides. Pile the cooked slices onto a warm serving dish and sprinkle with the cinnamon sugar. Serve with a jam sauce, made by gently melting some jam in a small saucepan and mixing with a little water.

Stale bread is transformed into a delicious rich dessert, not unlike French toast. One theory suggests the name came about because the pudding was served to retired military officers at Windsor Castle as payment for officiating at services and ceremonies.

Rhubarb hat

SERVES 4-6

Butter, for greasing
90g (3oz) breadcrumbs
30g (1oz) vegetable suet
60g (2oz) caster sugar
½ tsp ground ginger
10g (½oz) stem ginger,
    chopped
240g (8½oz) fresh
    rhubarb, chopped
Custard, to serve

For the suet pastry
240g (8½oz) self-raising
    flour, plus extra for
    dusting
Pinch of salt
120g (4oz) vegetable suet

GREASE A 1.1-LITRE (2-pint) pudding basin. To make the suet pastry, sift the flour and salt into a mixing bowl, add the suet and mix with enough cold water to form a fairly stiff dough. Divide the pastry into two thirds and one third. Roll out the larger piece on a floured surface and use to line the greased basin. Reserve the smaller piece for the lid.

TO MAKE THE FILLING, combine the breadcrumbs, suet, sugar and both types of ginger. Place half of the chopped rhubarb into the base of the lined basin. Cover with half of the breadcrumb mixture and repeat with the rest of the rhubarb, then the remaining crumbs.

ON THE FLOURED SURFACE, roll out the smaller piece of pastry and place on top of the pudding, wetting the edges to make it stick. Cover securely with a lid or foil and steam for 2–3 hours. Turn out and serve with custard.

Victoria's pudding

SERVES 6–8

60g (2oz) stoned dates
60g (2oz) demerara sugar
30g (1oz) glacé cherries,
    chopped
180g (6½oz) raisins
Pinch of ground nutmeg
¼ tsp mixed spice
2 tsp honey
2 tsp rum
120ml (4fl oz) cold tea
Butter, for greasing
90g (3oz) wholemeal
    self-raising flour
60g (2oz) wholemeal
    breadcrumbs
2 tbsp sunflower oil
1 small banana, peeled
    and mashed
1 egg, beaten
Custard, to serve

IN A LARGE MIXING BOWL, mix together the first nine listed ingredients, from the dates to the cold tea. Cover and leave to steep, ideally overnight or for at least a few hours.

THOROUGHLY GREASE A 1.1-LITRE (2-pint) pudding basin. Combine the remaining ingredients and mix into the steeped mixture until everything is well incorporated. Pour into the greased basin, cover with a lid or foil and steam for 5½ hours, adding more boiling water as necessary. Serve with custard.

It's a well-known fact that Queen Victoria loved puddings. And nobody would expect her namesake pudding to be frugal —loaded with dates, cherries, spices, rum and bananas, it's a pudding fit for a queen. This keeps very well and can be reheated by steaming for 1½ hours.

Prince Albert pudding

SERVES 6

270g (9½oz) prunes
180g (6½oz) unsalted butter, softened
120g (4oz) caster sugar
3 eggs, separated
45g (1½oz) ground rice
120g (4oz) brown breadcrumbs
Finely grated zest of 1 unwaxed lemon
Milk, to mix
Cream or custard, to serve

LINE THE BASE OF A 1.5-LITRE (2½-pint) pudding basin with a circle of greaseproof paper. Slice the prunes in half, removing the stones. Melt 60g (2oz) of the butter in a small saucepan, then dip the prune halves into the melted butter and use them to completely line the basin, placing the fleshy side against the basin's edge.

IN A MIXING BOWL, cream together the rest of the butter with the sugar until pale and fluffy. Beat in the egg yolks and fold in the ground rice, breadcrumbs and lemon zest. Mix with enough milk to reach a soft dropping consistency.

IN A CLEAN BOWL, beat the egg whites to a stiff froth, fold into the pudding mixture and spoon it carefully into the prune-lined basin. Cover securely with a lid or foil and steam for 2½ hours. Turn out and serve with cream or custard.

Like Queen Victoria, it seems husband Albert was also partial to a pudding or two, and this is just one of many bespoke puds that were probably invented in the palace kitchens especially for them.

FORGOTTEN PUDDINGS

Charlotte royale

SERVES 8

Butter, for greasing
500ml (18fl oz) milk
2 tsp vanilla essence
5 egg yolks
150g (5oz) caster sugar,
    plus extra for the basin
25g (1oz) gelatine leaves
500ml (18fl oz) whipping
    cream
Cream, to serve

For the Swiss roll
4 eggs
220g (8oz) caster sugar
120g (4oz) self-raising
    flour, sifted
200g (7oz) raspberry
    or strawberry jam

FIRST MAKE THE SWISS ROLL. Preheat the oven to 220°C (425°F), Gas Mark 7. Use greaseproof paper to line a shallow, oblong baking tray of approx. 45 x 20cm (18 x 8in). Whisk the eggs and 120g (4oz) of the sugar in a large heatproof bowl set over a saucepan of simmering water (a bain-marie) until thick, creamy and white in colour. Remove from the heat then gently fold the sifted flour into the mixture. Pour into the lined tray and level out. Bake for approximately 8 minutes or until firm to the touch.

SPREAD THE REMAINING 100g (3½oz) of caster sugar on a clean tea towel and carefully turn the sponge out of the tin while still warm, onto the sugared cloth. Spread the jam evenly over the sponge, then carefully roll up to form a Swiss roll. Trim the ends and leave to cool.

GREASE A 1.7-LITRE (3-pint) pudding basin and coat with caster sugar. Thinly slice the Swiss roll and arrange the slices inside the basin so that it is completely lined.

TO MAKE THE FILLING, heat the milk and vanilla essence in a saucepan and bring to the boil. Whisk together the egg yolks and sugar in a large mixing bowl until thick and creamy. Gradually pour the hot milk onto the egg and sugar mixture, whisking to combine. Then return the mixture to the saucepan and heat gradually until it thickens and will coat the back of a spoon; this should take 5–10 minutes.

SOAK THE GELATINE in cold water until soft, then remove and squeeze out any excess water. Add to the filling and stir until dissolved. Strain the mixture through a sieve and leave to cool. Whip the cream lightly, then fold into the filling just before it reaches setting point. Pour into the basin, and place in the fridge for 2 hours to set. Turn out onto a plate and serve with cream.

College pudding

SERVES 4–6

Butter, for greasing
120g (4oz) self-raising flour
Pinch of salt
120g (4oz) breadcrumbs
120g (4oz) vegetable suet
120g (4oz) raisins
60g (2oz) currants
30g (1oz) chopped mixed
   candied peel
90g (3oz) soft light
   brown sugar
1 egg, beaten
Approx. 6 tbsp milk
Custard, to serve

GREASE A 1.1-LITRE (2-pint) pudding basin. Sift the flour and salt together into a mixing bowl, then add the breadcrumbs, suet, dried fruit, candied peel and sugar and mix to combine. Stir in the beaten egg and enough of the milk to produce a soft dropping consistency.

SPOON INTO THE PUDDING BASIN, cover securely with a lid or foil and steam for 2½ hours. This pudding turns out easily if left to rest for a few minutes after taking it out of the steamer. Serve with custard.

So-called because it was traditionally served to students in the college halls of Oxford and Cambridge. A 1617 recipe for this pudding may be the earliest mention of suet in British cookery.

SERVES 6–8

Three and three pudding

170g (6oz) rough puff pastry

3 large cooking apples

85g (3oz) caster sugar,
plus 1 extra tablespoon
for the meringue

85g (3oz) unsalted butter,
plus extra for greasing

3 eggs, separated

Grated zest and juice
of 1 unwaxed lemon

Candied fruits, to decorate

Cream, to serve

PREHEAT THE OVEN TO 190°C (375°F), Gas Mark 5. Grease a 20cm (8in) pie dish and line with the puff pastry (see page 11). Decorate the edges with leaves and flowers cut from the trimmings.

PEEL AND CORE THE APPLES, cut into quarters and halve each piece again, then place in a saucepan with 1 tablespoon of water. Over a medium heat, simmer gently until soft, then remove from the heat and push the softened apple through a sieve, or purée in the pan with a hand blender.

ADD THE SUGAR, butter, egg yolks, lemon juice and zest to the puréed apple and mix well in the pan over a low heat for a few minutes until thick, but do not allow to boil. Transfer this mixture into the uncooked pastry case and bake for 30 minutes.

MEANWHILE, IN A SCRUPULOUSLY clean bowl, whisk the egg whites to stiff peaks, then add 1 tablespoon of sugar and whisk in well. Pile the meringue mixture onto the cooked fruit base, spreading it right to the edges to seal. Decorate with candied fruits and bake for a further 20 minutes at the bottom of the oven. Serve with cream.

Those with sharp eyes will understand the name of this pudding. Of course, it becomes much more mysterious when the ingredients are given in metric...

FORGOTTEN PUDDINGS

Apple dappy

SERVES 6–8

240g (8½oz) self-raising
    flour, plus extra
    for dusting
1 tsp baking powder
60g (2oz) unsalted butter,
    plus extra for greasing
150ml (5fl oz) milk
480g (1lb 1oz) cooking
    apples, peeled, cored
    and diced
1 tbsp demerara sugar
½ tsp ground allspice
    or cinnamon
Custard or clotted cream,
    to serve

For the lemon syrup
1 unwaxed lemon
1 tbsp golden syrup
15g (½oz) unsalted butter
120g (4oz) caster sugar

FIRST, MAKE THE LEMON SYRUP. Peel the lemon as thinly as possible and squeeze out the juice. Put the peel, juice and other syrup ingredients into a small saucepan with 200ml (7fl oz) water and heat gently, stirring until the sugar is dissolved. Leave to stand until needed.

PREHEAT THE OVEN TO 190°C (375°F), Gas Mark 5. Thoroughly grease a baking tin or ovenproof baking dish. Sift the flour and baking powder into a food processor, add the butter and process to fine breadcrumbs. (Alternatively, put in a large mixing bowl and rub together with your fingertips until they resemble breadcrumbs.) Mix in the milk to form a dough.

ROLL OUT THE DOUGH on a floured surface to a 20cm (8in) square, approx. 5mm (¼in) thick. Spread the chopped apples onto the dough and sprinkle with the sugar and spice. Roll up very tightly like a Swiss roll and cut into 2.5cm (1in) slices.

ARRANGE THE SLICES in the greased baking tin or dish in a single layer. Remove the peel from the syrup and pour over the slices. Bake in the oven for 30 minutes, or until the slices are puffed up and golden brown. Serve with custard or clotted cream.

The dappy hails from the West Country, where apples are grown in abundance throughout Dorset, Somerset, Devon and Cornwall for the local cider trade.

Apple bolster

SERVES 4–6

Butter, for greasing

225g (8oz) self-raising flour, plus extra for dusting

½ tsp salt

100g (3½oz) shredded suet

Approx. 135ml (4½fl oz) milk, plus 1 tbsp for brushing

450g (1lb) cooking apples

50g (2oz) soft light brown sugar

50g (2oz) sultanas

¼ tsp mixed spice

¼ tsp ground cinnamon

Custard or cream, to serve

PREHEAT THE OVEN TO 200°C (400°F), Gas Mark 6 and grease a baking tray. Stir the flour, salt and suet together in a large bowl. Gradually mix in enough milk to form a soft dough. Turn out the dough onto a floured surface and knead lightly before rolling out to a 30cm (12in) square.

PEEL AND CORE THE APPLES and cut the flesh into small pieces. Mix the apple with the sugar, sultanas and spices and arrange on the suet pastry to 2.5cm (1in) from the edges. Dampen the edges of the pastry with a little water, roll up tightly like a Swiss roll and seal the ends.

PUT THE PUDDING onto the greased baking tray with the seam facing downwards. Brush the surface with the remaining tablespoon of milk and bake in the oven for 40 minutes. Serve hot with custard or cream.

Cabinet pudding

SERVES 6

40g (1½oz) chopped
  mixed candied peel
25g (1oz) sultanas
100g (3½oz) currants
275g (10oz) ready-made
  sponge cake
50g (2oz) unsalted butter,
  plus extra for greasing
3 eggs
Approx. 450ml (16fl oz) milk
25g (1oz) caster sugar
Grated zest of
  1 unwaxed lemon
Pinch of ground nutmeg
Custard, to serve

THOROUGHLY GREASE A 1.1-LITRE (2-pint) pudding basin. Sprinkle the base with the candied peel, sultanas and a few of the currants. Try to get some of the fruit to stick to the sides of the basin. Cut the sponge cake into thin slices and arrange in layers in the basin, with currants and a little butter between each layer.

BREAK THE EGGS into a measuring jug and make up to 600ml (1 pint) with milk. Add the sugar, lemon zest and nutmeg and beat together until well mixed. Pour this liquid into the pudding basin very slowly, so that it soaks into the sponge cake. Leave to stand for 2 hours for the sponge to soak and soften.

COVER THE BASIN with a lid or double layer of greaseproof paper and steam the pudding for 1½ hours, keeping the water topped up as necessary. Remove from the pan and leave to stand for 3 minutes, then turn out onto a warmed serving plate. Serve warm with custard.

A traditional steamed pud with layers of sponge and lots of dried fruit, this is also sometimes called chancellor's pudding, or if served cold it is known as diplomat's pudding.

FORGOTTEN PUDDINGS

Sussex pond pudding

SERVES 8

120g (4oz) unsalted butter, plus extra for greasing
120g (4oz) demerara sugar
1 large lemon (preferably with a thin skin)
Custard, to serve

For the suet pastry
240g (8½oz) self-raising flour, plus extra for dusting
Pinch of salt
120g (4oz) vegetable suet
Approx. 150ml (5fl oz) mixed milk and water

GREASE A 1.5–1.7-LITRE (2½–3-pint) pudding basin. To make the pastry, sift the flour and salt into a mixing bowl, then add the suet and mix well. Add enough of the milk mixture to form a soft dough that can be rolled out. It is very important that the dough is not too wet.

ON A FLOURED SURFACE, roll the dough into a large circle, ensuring it's not rolled too thinly. Cut out a quarter of the circle and set aside to use later for making a lid. Place the remaining dough in the greased basin and join up the two cut edges, wetting them to seal, so that the basin is completely lined.

CUT THE BUTTER INTO SMALL PIECES and put half in the basin with half the sugar. Prick the lemon all over, using a thick skewer. Place on top of the butter and sugar in the basin. Cover with the rest of the butter and sugar.

RE-ROLL THE REMAINING PASTRY to make a lid. Wet the edges, fit over the filling and press the edges down to seal them firmly. Cover securely with a lid or foil and steam for 3½ hours (or longer for a really tender lemon), adding more water if needed. Turn out and serve with custard.

Kentish well pudding

SERVES 8

1 tbsp golden syrup

Grated zest and juice
of 1 unwaxed lemon

120g (4oz) unsalted butter,
plus extra for greasing

120g (4oz) soft light
brown sugar

120g (4oz) currants

Custard, to serve

For the suet pastry

240g (8½oz) self-raising
flour, plus extra for
dusting

Pinch of salt

120g (4oz) vegetable suet

Approx. 150ml (5fl oz)
mixed milk and water

GREASE A 1.5–1.7-LITRE (2½–3-pint) pudding basin. To make the pastry, sift the flour and salt into a mixing bowl, then add the suet and mix well. Add enough of the milk mixture to make a soft dough that can be rolled out. It is very important that the dough is not too wet.

ON A FLOURED SURFACE, roll the dough into a large circle, ensuring it's not rolled too thinly. Cut out a quarter of the circle and set aside to use later for making a lid.

PLACE THE GOLDEN SYRUP in the bottom of the greased basin, along with half the lemon zest. Wet the cut edges of the large piece of dough and place it in the greased basin, joining up the two cut edges so that the basin is completely lined. Cut the butter into small pieces, mix with the sugar and currants and place in the lined basin.

ON THE FLOURED SURFACE, roll out the remaining pastry to make a lid. Wet the edges, place over the filling and press the edges together to seal them firmly. Cover securely with a lid or foil and steam for 3½ hours. Turn out and serve with custard.

FORGOTTEN PUDDINGS

The lesser-known cousin of the Sussex pond pudding (see page 101), it's no surprise that Kent developed a similar pud, since the two counties share a border. Where the Sussex variety conceals a whole lemon, this recipe has a buttery centre filled with currants.

Bakewell pudding

SERVES 4–6

2 heaped tbsp apricot jam

3 eggs, beaten

90g (3oz) caster sugar

120g (4oz) unsalted butter, melted, plus extra for greasing

90g (3oz) ground almonds

Custard or cream, to serve

For the pastry

180g (6½oz) self-raising flour, plus extra for dusting

45g (1½oz) unsalted butter

45g (1½oz) lard

Iced water, to mix

PREHEAT THE OVEN TO 200°C (400°F), Gas Mark 6. Make the pastry by rubbing the flour, butter and lard together with your fingertips until the mixture resembles breadcrumbs. Add ice-cold water a tablespoonful at a time, until the crumbs come together to form a dough. Wrap in cling film and chill for 30 minutes, then roll out on a floured board to 5mm (¼in) thick.

GREASE A 20cm (8in) pie dish and line with the pastry (see page 11). Warm the jam gently in a saucepan or the microwave and spread this evenly over the uncooked pastry base. Beat the eggs and sugar together until pale and creamy, then stir in the melted butter and ground almonds and pour the mixture over the jam. Bake for 25–30 minutes or until the filling is set. Serve with custard or cream.

Bakewell pudding is the original confection for which the Derbyshire town became famous (not Bakewell tart!). If you walk along the high street today, you'll see signs in numerous tearoom and bakery windows, all of which claim to be the establishment responsible for the pudding's invention. Nobody knows which is telling the truth…

Nottingham batter pudding

SERVES 4

200g (7oz) plain flour

Pinch of salt

2 eggs

110ml (4fl oz) milk

50g (2oz) unsalted butter, softened, plus extra for greasing

50g (2oz) soft light brown sugar

Pinch of ground nutmeg

Pinch of ground cinnamon

4 evenly-sized Bramley apples

Custard or cream, to serve

SIFT THE FLOUR AND SALT into a mixing bowl. Measure 110ml (4fl oz) water in a jug, then add the eggs and milk and stir well to mix. Pour this into the flour and whisk very well until creamy and bubbly. Chill the batter in the fridge for a minimum of 30 minutes.

PREHEAT THE OVEN TO 200°C (400°F), Gas Mark 6 and grease an ovenproof baking dish, about 5cm (2in) deep. In a mixing bowl, cream together the butter and sugar until pale and fluffy, then beat in a pinch each of nutmeg and cinnamon.

CORE THE APPLES and fill them equally with the creamed mixture. Take the chilled batter from the fridge and beat well. Place the apples upright in the greased dish and pour the batter over the top. Bake in the oven for 45–50 minutes. Serve with custard or cream.

Nottinghamshire is famous for its Bramley Seedling apples, which have been growing there for over two centuries. So it follows that the Bramley apple is the central ingredient in this recipe for Nottingham's best-known pudding.

FORGOTTEN PUDDINGS

Blackberry Exeter pudding

SERVES 4–6

Butter, for greasing
90g (3oz) breadcrumbs
60g (2oz) caster sugar
30g (1oz) vegetable suet
120g (4oz) blackberries
120g (4oz) peeled, chopped
    cooking apple
Custard, to serve

For the suet pastry
240g (8½oz) self-raising
    flour, plus extra for
    dusting
Pinch of salt
120g (4oz) vegetable suet

GREASE A 1.1-LITRE (2-pint) pudding basin. To make the suet pastry, sift the flour and salt into a mixing bowl, add the suet and mix with enough cold water to form a fairly stiff dough, then divide the pastry into two thirds and one third. Roll out the larger piece on a floured surface and use to line the greased basin. Reserve the smaller piece for the lid.

TO MAKE THE FILLING, combine the breadcrumbs, sugar and suet. Place half the blackberries and chopped apple into the base of the lined basin. Cover with half the breadcrumb mixture and top with the remaining blackberries and apple. Cover with the rest of the crumbs.

ROLL OUT THE SMALLER PIECE OF PASTRY and place on top of the pudding, wetting the edges to make it stick. Cover securely with a lid or foil and steam for 2½–3 hours. Turn out and serve with custard.

A few years ago, Rick Stein featured The Pudding Club as one of his 'food heroes' on his TV series of the same name. This was the long-forgotten pudding that we chose to showcase to the nation on the programme.

Manchester puddings

MAKES 6

600ml (1 pint) milk

Grated zest of
1 unwaxed lemon

50g (2oz) unsalted butter

275g (10oz) caster sugar

100g (3½oz) white
breadcrumbs

4 eggs, separated,
plus 2 yolks

4 tsp good-quality
raspberry jam

PREHEAT THE OVEN TO 180°C (350°F), Gas Mark 4 and place six ovenproof 8cm (3in) ramekins into a deep baking tray. Pour the milk into a saucepan, add the lemon zest and place over a medium heat. Bring to the boil, to infuse, then remove from the heat and leave to cool for 10–15 minutes.

WHEN COOL, ADD THE BUTTER AND 50g (2oz) of the sugar to the lemon-infused milk, and heat gently for 4 minutes. Remove from the heat, add the breadcrumbs and mix well. Stir in the six egg yolks.

DIVIDE THE MIXTURE between the ramekins, then pour water into the baking tray so that it comes about halfway up the side of the ramekins. Place in the oven, taking care not to spill the water, and bake for 30 minutes. Remove from the oven and set aside to cool slightly. Increase the oven temperature to 220°C (425°F), Gas Mark 7.

TO MAKE THE MERINGUE, whisk the egg whites in a scrupulously clean bowl until they form soft peaks, then add the remaining 225g (8oz) of caster sugar and whisk to form stiff peaks.

PLACE A TEASPOON OF RASPBERRY JAM onto each pudding, then spoon a generous amount of meringue onto the top of each. Return the puddings to the hot oven and bake for approximately 10 minutes until slightly browned. Serve while still hot.

Light cloutie dumpling

SERVES 8

360g (12½oz) self-raising
   flour
½ tsp salt
180g (6½oz) unsalted
   butter, plus extra
   for greasing
120g (4oz) soft light
   brown sugar
1 tsp ground cinnamon
1 tsp ground ginger
Finely grated zest
   of 1 orange
480g (1lb 1oz) sultanas
240g (8½oz) currants
1 tbsp golden syrup
1 tbsp black treacle
2 eggs, beaten
Milk, to mix
Custard to serve

GREASE A 1.7-LITRE (3-pint) pudding basin. Sift the flour and salt together into a mixing bowl, then rub in the butter with your fingertips until the mixture resembles crumbs. Stir in the sugar, spices, orange zest and dried fruits.

MAKE A WELL IN THE CENTRE OF THE MIXTURE and pour in the syrup, treacle and eggs, then mix with enough milk to make a stiff but moist mixture. Spoon into the greased basin, cover securely with a lid or foil and steam for 3 hours. Turn out and serve with custard.

This Scottish suet pudding is named after the cloth ('cloutie') in which it was originally cooked. Traditionally, any leftovers were kept and re-heated by frying them in a little butter.

SERVES 4–6

Scottish flummery

1 tbsp oatmeal (ideally pinhead)
300ml (11fl oz) double cream
3 tbsp clear honey
4 tbsp liqueur whisky (Drambuie)
Juice of ½ lemon

HEAT THE OATMEAL GENTLY in a heavy-based saucepan until it just turns brown, then remove from the heat and set aside. In a large bowl, beat the cream until smooth but not stiff.

MELT THE HONEY GENTLY in a saucepan until it runs easily, being careful not to let it boil. Fold the melted honey into the beaten cream, then stir in the liqueur and lemon juice. Spoon into individual glasses or bowls and serve while still warm, with the browned oatmeal sprinkled on top.

Legend has it that Flora Macdonald made this pudding for Bonnie Prince Charlie when she helped him flee Scotland and escape to the Isle of Skye.

PUDDINGS
WITH A TWIST

CHAPTER 5

British cuisine has always welcomed new ideas and exotic
flavours and our puddings are no exception. In this chapter,
some of the most classic British puds are customised using
different ingredients and fresh combinations, to offer
delicious twists on familiar recipes. The Eton mess is
reinvented with blackberries, carrots make a wonderfully
moist pudding that will rival any cake, and the roly poly
is updated to include lemon curd. Impress your friends with
an unusual blackcurrant and mint pie, or try our flavourful
rosemary syllabub (it may seem modern, but is in fact
centuries old!). Why not have fun inventing your own
twists on other classic recipes throughout this book?

Rosemary syllabub

SERVES 6–8

1 large, fresh rosemary
    sprig, plus extra
    to garnish
4 tbsp dry white wine
4 tbsp brandy
Grated zest and juice
    of 2 unwaxed lemons,
    plus extra to garnish
120g (4oz) caster sugar
500ml (18fl oz) double
    cream

REMOVE CLUMPS OF ROSEMARY LEAVES from the woody stem and bruise them well. Put the leaves in a bowl and cover with the wine and brandy. Add the lemon juice, zest and sugar. Leave to steep overnight or for a minimum of a few hours to allow the full flavour of the rosemary to infuse.

STRAIN THE INFUSED WINE MIXTURE into a large bowl and stir the cream into the infusion. Whip until thick but not stiff and pour into serving glasses. Serve chilled, garnished with lemon zest and rosemary. Eat within 24 hours or the syllabub may separate.

Variation

As an alternative to rosemary, you can try lemon geranium leaves, rose petals, elderflowers, lavender or sweet cicely. Simply infuse the wine and lemon juice with your chosen flavour in the same way as described.

The syllabub can be traced back to medieval times and for centuries remained one of the most popular and common desserts in Britain, until the end of the Victorian era saw the arrival of ice cream. Whilst rosemary might seem an unusual ingredient here, it is actually very authentic.

Quince amber

SERVES 4-6

450g (1lb) peeled,
  cored quinces
50g (2oz) unsalted butter,
  plus extra for greasing
200g (7oz) caster sugar
225g (8oz) fresh
  white bread
3 eggs, separated

PREHEAT THE OVEN TO 180°C (350°F), Gas Mark 4 and thoroughly grease a 20cm (8in) pie dish. Quarter the quinces and cut each piece in half again. Place in a saucepan with the butter and 50g (2oz) of the sugar. Cook over a gentle heat until the fruit mixture is soft and thick.

PROCESS THE BREAD into fine breadcrumbs and stir into the fruit mixture, then beat in the egg yolks. Pour the mixture into the greased dish and bake in the oven for 30 minutes.

MEANWHILE, IN A SCRUPULOUSLY clean bowl, whisk the egg whites to stiff peaks. Add half the remaining sugar and whisk until the mixture is thick and shiny. Fold in the remaining sugar with a metal spoon and pile the meringue onto the cooked fruit base. Return to the oven and bake for another 10 minutes. Serve immediately.

The quince is a large fruit related to apples and pears, which has been enjoying renewed popularity in recent years. Yellow when raw and pink when cooked, its season is short (look for them between October and December) and they are more likely to be found at farmers' markets than in your local supermarket. The name of this pudding comes from the beautiful golden colour of the toasted meringue.

PUDDINGS WITH A TWIST

Lord Randall's pudding

SERVES 4–6

225g (8oz) dried apricots, chopped

225g (8oz) thick-cut Seville orange marmalade

225g (8oz) plain flour

1 tsp bicarbonate of soda

225g (8oz) unsalted butter, softened, plus extra for greasing

120g (4oz) soft dark brown sugar

1 large egg, beaten

90ml (3fl oz) milk

Custard, to serve

LIGHTLY GREASE A 1.1-LITRE (2-pint) pudding basin and cover the bottom with a little of the chopped apricots and marmalade. Sift together the flour and bicarbonate of soda into a large bowl.

IN A MIXING BOWL, cream together the butter and sugar until pale and fluffy. One at a time, add the beaten egg, milk, sifted flour and soda, and remaining apricots to the creamed mixture, stirring well after each addition. Beat vigorously and finally mix in the rest of the marmalade.

POUR THE MIXTURE into the greased basin and cover securely with a lid or foil. Steam for 1½–2 hours. Turn out and serve with custard.

This recipe came to us 20 years ago as a competition entry, although the winner couldn't explain the name, as it was passed down from her late grandmother. It's probably inspired by a Victorian ballad (made popular by Steeleye Span in the 1980s), in which Lord Randall laments to his mother that he's been poisoned by 'eels fried in a pan' (so our pudding wasn't to blame!). This is the name of one of our themed Pudding Rooms, where you can sleep soundly in the knowledge that Lord Randall is watching over you.

Tutti-frutti pudding

SERVES 4–6

2½ tbsp golden syrup

120g (4oz) unsalted butter, softened, plus extra for greasing

120g (4oz) caster sugar

Finely grated zest and juice of 1 orange

2 eggs

90g (3oz) self-raising flour, sifted

60g (2oz) breadcrumbs

60g (2oz) stoned prunes, finely chopped

60g (2oz) dried apricots, finely chopped

60g (2oz) red glacé cherries, finely chopped

30g (1oz) green glacé cherries or angelica, finely chopped

Custard, to serve

GREASE A 1.1-LITRE (2-pint) pudding basin and cover the bottom with the golden syrup. In a mixing bowl, cream together the butter and sugar until pale and fluffy, then stir in the grated orange zest. Beat the eggs and gradually add them to the mixture.

MIX THE SIFTED FLOUR with the breadcrumbs and fold lightly into the pudding mixture. Fold in the prunes, apricots, cherries and angelica, along with the orange juice. Stir well so that the ingredients are fully incorporated. Pour into the greased basin, cover securely with a lid or foil and steam for 2 hours. Turn out and serve with custard.

Prune and muscat puddings

MAKES 6

Melted butter, for greasing

24 pitted prunes
(about 250g/9oz)

375ml (13fl oz) muscat
or port

100g (3½oz) caster sugar

175g (6oz) unsalted butter,
at room temperature

100g (3½oz) dark brown
muscovado sugar

2 eggs

2 tbsp milk

85g (3oz) ground almonds

40g (1½oz) plain flour

40g (1½oz) self-raising flour

½ tsp mixed spice

Vanilla ice cream, to serve

PREHEAT THE OVEN TO 180°C (350°F), Gas Mark 4.
Brush six ramekins or individual 200ml (7fl oz)
pudding basins with melted butter and line the base
of each with a circle of non-stick baking parchment.

PLACE THE PRUNES, MUSCAT AND 250ml (9fl oz)
water into a large saucepan over a medium heat and
bring to a simmer. Cook for 10 minutes or until the
prunes are soft. Lift out the prunes with a slotted
spoon and place in a medium-sized heatproof bowl.

ADD THE CASTER SUGAR to the saucepan of prune
liquid and cook, stirring, for 3 minutes or until the
sugar dissolves. Bring to a simmer and cook for 10
minutes or until the syrup thickens — you need about
190ml (6½fl oz) syrup. Pour the syrup over the
prunes in the bowl.

IN A LARGE MIXING BOWL, beat the butter and
brown sugar with an electric hand mixer until pale
and creamy. Add the eggs one at a time, beating well
after each addition. Stir in the milk and fold in the
ground almonds, both types of flour and the mixed
spice until well mixed.

PLACE FOUR PRUNES in the bottom of each
ramekin or basin, in a single layer. Add 2 teaspoons
of syrup to each ramekin to cover the prunes. Reserve
any remaining syrup. Spoon the sponge mixture into
the ramekins and smooth the surface with the back of
the spoon. Cover each ramekin with lightly greased
foil and place them in a roasting tin. Pour enough

(continued overleaf)

PUDDINGS WITH A TWIST

(continued from previous page)

boiling water into the tin to reach halfway up the sides of the ramekins.

BAKE FOR 40 MINUTES or until an inserted skewer comes out clean. Remove the ramekins carefully from the roasting tin and set aside for 5 minutes to cool slightly before turning the puddings out onto serving plates. Serve with vanilla ice cream and drizzle the puddings with any remaining syrup.

COOKING TIME
30–40 MINUTES

Butterscotch tart

SERVES 8

375g (13 oz) shortcrust pastry (see page 10), chilled
320g (11½oz) unsalted butter
320g (11½oz) demerara sugar
180ml (6½fl oz) milk
80g (3oz) plain flour, plus extra for dusting
Cold whipped cream, to serve

ROLL OUT THE CHILLED PASTRY on a floured surface, to 5mm (¼in) thickness, and use it to line a 30cm (12in) tart dish (see page 11). Refrigerate for 30 minutes, then preheat the oven to 190°C (400°F), Gas Mark 5 and blind bake the pastry case for 25 minutes (see page 11). Remove from the oven and set aside.

MELT THE BUTTER IN A SAUCEPAN over a low heat and mix in the demerara sugar until dissolved. Mix a little milk with the flour to form a paste; add this slowly to the butter and sugar in the pan, along with the remaining milk. Gradually heat the mixture, whisking continuously until the butterscotch coats the back of a spoon.

POUR THE BUTTERSCOTCH into the cooked pastry case and allow to cool before refrigerating. Serve cold with cold whipped cream.

Lime meringue pie

SERVES 6–8

375g (13 oz) shortcrust
pastry (see page 10),
chilled
Flour, for dusting
110g (4oz) unsalted butter
Grated zest of 4 limes
and juice of 8
8 eggs, separated
4 tsp cornflour
400g (14oz) caster sugar

ROLL OUT THE CHILLED PASTRY on a floured surface, to 5mm (¼in) thickness and use it to line a 30cm (12in) tart dish (see page 11). Refrigerate for 30 minutes, then preheat the oven to 200°C (400°F), Gas Mark 6 and blind bake the pastry case for 20 minutes (see page 11). Remove from the oven and set aside.

TO PREPARE THE FILLING, melt the butter in a saucepan over a low heat, add the lime zest and juice and gently heat through. Whisk the egg yolks in a bowl until pale and creamy. Slowly add the melted butter and lime mixture to the yolks, whisking continuously until well combined. Pour the mixture back into the saucepan.

MIX THE CORNFLOUR with a little water to form a paste, add this to the lime and yolk mixture and continue to cook over a low heat, stirring continuously until the mixture thickens. Set aside until needed.

WHISK THE EGG WHITES in a scrupulously clean bowl until they form soft peaks, then gradually add the caster sugar, whisking until stiff peaks form. Spoon the lime mixture into the cooked pastry case and top with the meringue. To brown the meringue, you can either place in the oven, preheated to 200°C (400°F), Gas Mark 6, for 10 minutes or use a kitchen blowtorch.

PUDDINGS WITH A TWIST

Lemon curd roly poly

SERVES 4–6

180g (6½oz) self-raising
   flour, plus extra for
   dusting
Pinch of salt
90g (3oz) vegetable suet
Finely grated zest of
   1 unwaxed lemon
Milk, to mix
450g (1lb) lemon curd
1 tbsp caster sugar
Custard, to serve

PREHEAT THE OVEN TO 190°C (375°F), Gas Mark 5. Sift the flour and salt together into a mixing bowl, then add the suet, lemon zest and enough milk to make a dough. Roll out the dough on a floured surface to about 25cm (10in) square and spread with the lemon curd. Dampen the edges of the dough with water and roll up like a Swiss roll.

PLACE THE ROLY POLY IN A ROASTING TIN and put in the oven, raising one side of the tin so that the pudding rolls to one end. This will prevent it from unravelling. Bake in the oven for 1 hour. (Alternatively, wrap in foil to hold its shape and in cling film to make it watertight. Steam for 1½ hours, then carefully remove the cling film and foil.) Sprinkle with the sugar and serve with custard.

*Make sure you buy the best
available lemon curd, or better
still, make your own!*

Lemon surprise pudding

SERVES 4

Grated zest and juice of
2 unwaxed lemons
75g (3oz) unsalted butter
150g (5oz) caster sugar
3 eggs, separated
75g (3oz) self-raising flour
450ml (16fl oz) milk

PREHEAT THE OVEN TO 200°C (400°F), Gas Mark 6 and thoroughly grease a deep, ovenproof baking dish. In a mixing bowl, beat the lemon zest, butter and sugar until pale and creamy. Add the egg yolks and flour and mix well. Gradually stir in the milk, along with 2–3 tablespoons of lemon juice.

IN A SCRUPULOUSLY CLEAN BOWL, whisk the egg whites until stiff, then fold them into the pudding mixture with a metal spoon. Pour the mixture into the greased dish. Stand the dish in a roasting tin and pour water into the tin to reach halfway up the outside of the dish.

BAKE IN THE OVEN FOR ABOUT 45 minutes until the top is set and spongy to the touch. The pudding will have separated into a custard layer underneath with a sponge topping. Serve immediately.

Millennium pudding

SERVES 4–6

Butter, for greasing
240g (8½oz) self-raising
   flour, plus extra
   for dusting
Pinch of salt
120g (4oz) vegetable suet
480g (1lb 1oz) fresh
   peaches, stoned and
   chopped
1 tbsp soft light brown sugar
Custard, to serve

For the lemon syrup
1 lemon
1 tbsp golden syrup
15g (½oz) unsalted butter
120g (4oz) soft light
   brown sugar

FIRST MAKE THE LEMON SYRUP. Peel the lemon as thinly as possible and squeeze out the juice. Put the rind, juice and remaining syrup ingredients into a saucepan, add 200ml (7fl oz) water and heat gently until the sugar has dissolved. Leave to stand until needed.

PREHEAT THE OVEN TO 190°C (375°F), Gas Mark 5 and grease a 1.1-litre (2-pint) ovenproof baking dish. Sift the flour and salt together into a mixing bowl, then add the suet and mix with enough water to create a firm dough.

ROLL OUT THE DOUGH on a floured surface to about 25cm (10in) square and 5mm (¼in) thick. Spread the chopped peaches and brown sugar evenly over the square and roll up, as you would a Swiss roll. Cut into 2.5cm (1in) slices and arrange flat in the greased dish with the fruit facing upwards.

REMOVE THE LEMON RIND from the syrup and pour the syrup over the slices in the dish. Bake in the oven for 30 minutes or until puffed up and golden brown. Serve with custard.

This recipe was a Pudding Club invention, to mark the beginning of the year 2000. We wanted to create a brand-new twist on the great British pudding that would see us into the 21st century.

Oriental ginger pudding

SERVES 4–6

Butter, for greasing

180g (6½oz) self-raising flour

Pinch of salt

2 tsp ground ginger

90g (3oz) vegetable suet

45g (1½oz) soft dark brown sugar

45g (1½oz) stem ginger, chopped

3 tbsp golden syrup, warmed, plus extra to serve

1 egg, beaten

Custard, to serve

LIGHTLY GREASE A 1.1-LITRE (2-pint) pudding basin. Sift together the flour, salt and ground ginger into a mixing bowl. Add the suet, sugar and chopped stem ginger and mix to combine, then add the warmed syrup and beaten egg and mix well.

POUR THE MIXTURE INTO THE GREASED BASIN, cover securely with a lid or foil and steam for 1½ hours. Turn out onto a warmed dish and serve with extra syrup and custard.

Another of our Pudding Rooms, where you can sleep under the watchful gaze of a fearsome ginger dragon. Although commonplace in many traditional British recipes, ginger is far from native to our shores. It appeared in Britain in the 1640s, imported from Asia, but was quickly adopted into our own cuisine.

PUDDINGS WITH A TWIST

Pear and ginger charlotte

SERVES 6

450g (1lb) Conference
  pears, peeled, cored
  and chopped
110g (4oz) unsalted butter
1 tbsp caster sugar
6 medium-thickness slices
  of bread, crusts removed
20g (¾oz) stem ginger,
  chopped
1 egg yolk
Cream or ice cream, to serve

PLACE THE CHOPPED PEARS in a saucepan with 25g (1oz) of the butter and the tablespoon of sugar. Cook over a low heat until soft and broken down. Remove from the heat and purée the pears in the pan with a hand blender. Leave to cool.

PREHEAT THE OVEN TO 180°C (350°F), Gas Mark 4. Melt the remaining 85g (3oz) of butter in a small saucepan, then brush it over one side of each bread slice, making sure the bread is well covered. Cut into rectangles and use most of them to line a 20–25cm (8–10in) pudding basin or round cake tin, 12cm (4½in) in depth, placing the pieces buttered-side down and slightly overlapping (reserve a little bread for the top). Press them on firmly.

WHEN THE PEAR PURÉE IS COOL, add the chopped stem ginger and whisk in the egg yolk, then pour the mixture into the bread-lined basin. Cover with the remaining sliced bread, butter-side up, and press down firmly. Bake in the oven for 45 minutes, until golden brown. Remove from the oven and carefully turn out onto a warm plate. Serve with cream or ice cream.

COOKING TIME
1–1½ HOURS

Coconut rice pudding

SERVES 4

60g (2oz) pudding rice
25g (1oz) golden caster sugar
300ml (11fl oz) skimmed milk
300ml (11fl oz) coconut milk
Fresh raspberries, to serve (optional)

PREHEAT THE OVEN TO 150 °C (300°F), Gas Mark 2. Put the rice, sugar, milk and coconut milk into a non-stick saucepan and gently bring to the boil, stirring occasionally so that the mixture doesn't stick to the pan.

POUR INTO AN OVENPROOF BAKING DISH with a lid and bake in the centre of the oven for 1–1½ hours, until creamy. Serve with fresh raspberries (when in season).

WHY NOT TRY...?
This is particularly delicious when served with a purée of fresh mango.

Carrot pudding

SERVES 4–6

Butter, for greasing
60g (2oz) self-raising flour
60g (2oz) breadcrumbs
30g (1oz) caster sugar
Pinch of salt
½ tsp mixed spice
60g (2oz) shredded suet
60g (2oz) chopped mixed
    candied peel
120g (4oz) mixed dried fruit
60g (2oz) raw carrot,
    peeled and grated
60g (2oz) raw potato,
    peeled and grated
2 tsp black treacle
Pinch of bicarbonate
    of soda
Orange juice, to mix
Custard, to serve

THOROUGHLY GREASE A 1.1-LITRE (2-pint) pudding basin. In the order listed, measure all the ingredients, except for the orange juice, into a large mixing bowl, mixing them together after every addition. (It is very important to mix them together in the order given.)

MIX WITH ENOUGH ORANGE JUICE to reach a dropping consistency, then pour the mixture into the pudding basin, cover with a lid or foil and steam for 2½–3 hours. Turn out onto a warmed plate and serve with custard.

An ancestor of the much-loved carrot cake, this pudding came about as a medieval response to the high price of sugar. The use of carrots in puddings and cakes became popular once again in the Second World War, when conventional sweeteners and sugars were heavily rationed.

Blackcurrant and mint pie

SERVES 6

450g (1lb) blackcurrants, topped and tailed

2½ tsp finely chopped mint

110g (4oz) caster sugar, plus extra for sprinkling

225g (8oz) shortcrust pastry (see page 10)

Plain flour, for dusting

Cream, to serve

PREHEAT THE OVEN TO 200°C (400°F), Gas Mark 6. Wash the blackcurrants in a colander and rinse several times under running water. Drain thoroughly and put them in a shallow 18–20cm (7–8in) pie dish or tin. Mix the chopped mint with the sugar and distribute evenly over the blackcurrants.

ROLL OUT THE SHORTCRUST PASTRY on a floured surface to a thickness of 5mm (¼in). Cover the filling with the pastry, pressing it onto the edges of the pie dish and decorating the top with pastry leaves or flowers made from the trimmings. With a sharp knife, cut a slit in the centre of the pastry top to allow steam to escape during cooking.

BRUSH THE PASTRY WITH WATER and sprinkle with a little extra caster sugar. Bake the pie on the middle shelf of the oven for 35–40 minutes or until golden. Serve the pie cold with fresh cream.

Blackberry Eton mess

SERVES 6

3 large egg whites

175g (6oz) golden
caster sugar

575ml (1 pint) double
or whipping cream

450g (1lb) fresh
blackberries (or frozen)

1 tbsp icing sugar

PREHEAT THE OVEN to a very low setting: approx.
130–140°C (250–275°F), Gas Mark ½–1. Line
a flat baking sheet with non-stick baking parchment.
To make the meringue, place the egg whites in a
scrupulously clean bowl and whisk until they form
soft peaks. Add the caster sugar gradually, a spoonful
at a time, whisking well between each addition until
the sugar is thoroughly incorporated.

SPOON THE MERINGUE onto the parchment and
spread out until about 2cm (¾in) thick. Place the
baking sheet in the oven for approximately 1 hour,
then turn off the heat and leave the meringue inside
the oven to dry out, until cold. The meringue can
then be used immediately or stored in an airtight
container until needed.

BREAK UP THE MERINGUE INTO 2cm (¾in)
pieces. In a large bowl, whip the cream until sloppy.
In another bowl, mix the blackberries with the icing
sugar. Combine all three ingredients – the meringue
pieces, cream and blackberries – and spoon into
glass bowls. Serve chilled.

*If you prefer a less sweet version of
this, you can use extra-thick natural
yoghurt instead of whipped cream.*

PUDDINGS WITH A TWIST

Rhubarb and orange brown Betty

SERVES 6

600g (1lb 5oz) chopped
    rhubarb
20g (¾oz) caster sugar
Grated zest and juice
    of 2 oranges
25g (1oz) demerara sugar
200g (7oz) crushed sweet
    biscuits (digestives
    or similar)
50g (2oz) breadcrumbs
50g (2oz) flaked or
    chopped nuts
50g (2oz) unsalted butter
Cream or ice cream, to serve

PREHEAT THE OVEN TO 175°C (340°F), Gas Mark 3–4. Mix together the chopped rhubarb, caster sugar, orange juice and half the zest, and place in a shallow, 20cm (8in) square, ovenproof baking dish. Combine the demerara sugar with the crushed biscuits, breadcrumbs and nuts and spread this over the rhubarb mix.

PLACE SMALL PIECES OF BUTTER across the top of the crumb mix. Bake in the oven for 30–40 minutes until the rhubarb is tender and cooked through and the crumb topping is crisp and brown. Serve with cream or ice cream.

Rhubarb roulade

SERVES 6-8

4 egg whites

325g (11½oz) caster sugar

1 tsp vanilla essence

1 tsp white wine or malt vinegar

1 tsp cornflour

500g (1lb 2oz) trimmed rhubarb, chopped into 3–5cm (1–2in) pieces

3 gelatine leaves

375ml (13fl oz) double cream, plus optional extra to serve

PREHEAT THE OVEN TO 160°C (325°F), Gas Mark 3. Cover a 25cm (10in) square baking sheet with non-stick baking parchment. In a scrupulously clean bowl, whisk the egg whites until they form soft peaks, then slowly add 200g (7oz) of the sugar while still whisking. Add the vanilla essence, vinegar and cornflour and whisk until the mixture is stiff.

SPREAD THE MERINGUE MIX EVENLY across the lined baking sheet and bake for 25 minutes. Remove from the oven and allow to cool before carefully removing the soft meringue from the parchment.

WHILE THE MERINGUE IS COOKING, place the chopped rhubarb in a medium saucepan with the remaining 125g (4½oz) of the sugar. Cook over a medium–high heat for about 15 minutes until the rhubarb is cooked and has broken down. Discard the liquid and allow the rhubarb to cool.

SOAK THE GELATINE LEAVES in cold water until soft. Remove the softened leaves from the water and place in a small saucepan with 125ml (4½fl oz) of the cream. Heat gently to dissolve the gelatine, then remove from the heat and allow this to cool for a few minutes. Whip the remaining cream to soft peaks.

MIX THE TWO CREAMS TOGETHER and carefully fold in the rhubarb. Refrigerate the mixture until it has begun to stiffen. Spread it evenly over the meringue and carefully roll up like a Swiss roll.

TO SERVE, slice and enjoy on its own or with cream.

PUDDINGS WITH A TWIST

Gooseberry and elderflower fool

SERVES 4–6

450g (1lb) gooseberries,
  topped and tailed
60g (2oz) granulated sugar
10 elderflower heads
1 thick strip of pared
  lemon rind
300ml (11fl oz) crème fraîche

PUT THE GOOSEBERRIES AND SUGAR in a large saucepan with 4 tablespoons of water and bring to the boil. Simmer gently until the fruit starts to soften.

SET ASIDE A FEW ELDERFLOWERS to use as a garnish, then tie the remaining elderflower heads in a muslin bag with the piece of lemon rind. Add this to the pan and continue to simmer gently for a further 15 minutes.

REMOVE THE ELDERFLOWER BAG from the pan, squeezing all of its juices into the mixture. Use a fork to roughly mash the gooseberry mixture. Set aside to cool.

DIVIDE ABOUT ONE QUARTER of the gooseberry purée among serving glasses. Fold the crème fraîche into the remaining gooseberry purée and add this to the glasses. Garnish each glass with the reserved elderflowers.

Greengage flapjack

SERVES 4–6

500g (1lb 2oz) greengages, stoned and halved

75g (3oz) caster sugar

90g (3oz) unsalted butter

90g (3oz) soft light brown sugar

1 tbsp golden syrup

120g (4oz) porridge oats

Custard or cream, to serve

PREHEAT THE OVEN TO 180°C (350°F), Gas Mark 4. Place the greengage halves in a shallow, ovenproof baking dish and sprinkle with the caster sugar.

PUT THE BUTTER, BROWN SUGAR and golden syrup in a saucepan and melt over a gentle heat. Stir in the oats. Spread this mixture over the greengages and bake in the oven for 30 minutes until the flapjack is brown and crisp on top. Serve with custard or cream.

If you can't find greengages, substitute with another tart fruit — damsons work well, as do gooseberries.

CHOCOHOLICS & NUTCASES

Definitely the most indulgent chapter in this book, these puddings fit the bill when something a bit special is called for. Certain treats here will go down very well with kids and adults alike, such as our squidgy chocolate pudding, oozing with chocolate sauce; whilst the more sophisticated hazelnut roulade or dark chocolate pavé will wow your dinner-party guests. Meanwhile, chocoholics will delight in discovering ways to introduce chocolate into other British classics, such as chocolate bread and butter pudding and a white chocolate and raspberry trifle.

Chestnut and chocolate pudding

SERVES 6

225g (8oz) unsalted butter,
   plus extra for greasing
100g (3½oz) dark
   chocolate, minimum 50%
   cocoa solids, broken up
225g (8oz) self-raising flour
5 tbsp cocoa powder
4 eggs, beaten
225g (8oz) golden
   caster sugar
180g (6½oz) cooked, peeled
   sweet chestnuts, chopped
½ tsp vanilla essence
Chocolate sauce (see page
   143), to serve
Cream or vanilla ice cream,
   to serve

LIGHTLY GREASE A 1.1-LITRE (2-pint) pudding basin. Put the butter and dark chocolate in a saucepan and melt over a low heat. Sift the flour and cocoa powder together into a bowl, then add to the melted chocolate. Stir in the beaten eggs, sugar, chestnuts and vanilla essence and mix well.

POUR THE PUDDING MIXTURE into the greased basin. Cover with a lid or foil and steam for 2–2½ hours. Turn out onto a plate and serve with extra chocolate sauce, and cream or vanilla ice cream.

It's important to use good-quality high-cocoa content chocolate to give this pudding a rich, deep flavour.

Very chocolate pudding

SERVES 4–6

200g (7oz) unsalted butter, softened, plus extra for greasing
200g (7oz) caster sugar
200g (7oz) self-raising flour
5 tbsp cocoa powder
3 eggs, beaten
60g (2oz) chocolate chips
Custard and chocolate sauce (see below), to serve

For the chocolate sauce
170g (6oz) chocolate, 50% cocoa solids, broken up
2–3 tsp caster sugar
125ml (4½fl oz) double cream

GREASE A 1.1-LITRE (2-pint) pudding basin. In a mixing bowl, cream together the butter and sugar until pale and fluffy. Sift the flour and cocoa together into a separate bowl, then add to the creamed mixture a little at a time, alternating with the beaten egg, and beating well after each addition. Finally, stir in half the chocolate chips.

COVER THE BASE OF THE GREASED BASIN with the remaining chocolate chips, then pour the sponge mixture on top. Cover with a lid or foil and steam for 1½ hours.

TO MAKE THE SAUCE place all the ingredients in a saucepan over a low heat until the chocolate has melted and the sugar has dissolved. Mix well together and remove from the heat. Turn the pudding out onto a plate and serve with custard and the chocolate sauce.

This chocolate sauce is very rich, so a little goes a long way. If you prefer it a little sweeter, add the third teaspoon of sugar (you can wait to taste the sauce before choosing whether or not to add this, but make sure to give it enough extra time over the heat for the additional sugar to dissolve). Any leftovers can be frozen for up to 2 months in a sealed rigid container. Defrost at room temperature for 2–3 hours or overnight in the fridge.

CHOCOHOLICS & NUTCASES

Squidgy chocolate puddings

MAKES 8

340g (12oz) unsalted
  butter, softened

340g (12oz) soft light
  brown sugar

6 eggs, beaten

280g (10oz) self-raising
  flour

70g (2½oz) cocoa powder

Extra chocolate topping
  (see below) to serve

Cream or vanilla ice cream,
  to serve

For the chocolate topping

170g (6oz) chocolate,
  70% cocoa solids

2 tsp caster sugar

125ml (4½fl oz) double
  cream

PLACE ALL THE TOPPING INGREDIENTS in a saucepan over a low heat until the chocolate has melted and the sugar has dissolved. Mix well and remove from the heat.

GREASE EIGHT 200ml (7fl oz) pudding basins. In a mixing bowl, cream the butter and sugar until pale and fluffy. Add the beaten eggs to the mixture – if the mixture separates, just stir in a little of the flour. Sift the remaining flour and cocoa powder together into a separate bowl, then fold them into the creamed mixture, stirring well to incorporate. Add a little water if the mixture seems dry.

PLACE ABOUT 1 HEAPED TABLESPOON of the chocolate topping into each 200ml (7fl oz) pudding basin. Divide the sponge mix evenly between the basins and seal with a lid or foil. Steam for 45–60 minutes. Serve with extra chocolate topping, and cream or vanilla ice cream.

This much-loved pudding was the inspiration for our Chocolate Suite, the most luxurious and popular of our themed Pudding Rooms. Where else can you sleep in a box of chocolates?

CHOCOHOLICS & NUTCASES

Prune and chocolate pudding

SERVES 6

60g (2oz) unsalted
   butter, softened
150g (5oz) caster sugar
1 egg, beaten
150g (5oz) self-raising flour
75g (3oz) cocoa powder
200g (7oz) chopped,
   pitted prunes
120ml (4fl oz) milk
Vanilla ice cream or
   whipped cream, to serve

For the sauce
100g (3½oz) dark chocolate,
   50% cocoa solids
50g (2oz) caster sugar

PREHEAT THE OVEN TO 170°C (325°F), Gas Mark 3. In a mixing bowl, cream together the butter and sugar until pale and fluffy. Gradually mix in the egg, then beat until well combined. Sift the flour and cocoa together and fold into the mixture, then add the chopped prunes and milk and mix well.

TO MAKE THE SAUCE, heat the chocolate, sugar and 240ml (8½fl oz) water in a saucepan over a low heat until the chocolate has melted. Pour the sauce into a deep, 1.1-litre (2-pint), ovenproof baking dish, pour the sponge mixture on top and level out. Bake in the oven for 50–60 minutes. Serve hot with vanilla ice cream or whipped cream.

Marbled pudding

SERVES 4–6

150g (5oz) self-raising flour

Pinch of salt

100g (3½oz) unsalted butter or margarine, softened, plus extra for greasing

100g (3½oz) caster sugar

2 eggs, beaten

Milk, to mix

Grated zest of 1 unwaxed lemon

2 tbsp good-quality cocoa powder

Chocolate sauce (see page 143) or custard, to serve

GREASE A 1.1-LITRE (2-pint) pudding basin. Sift the flour and salt into a bowl. In a mixing bowl, cream together the butter and sugar until pale and fluffy, then add the egg a little at a time, beating well after each addition. Fold in half the flour with a metal spoon, then repeat with the rest. Add milk a little at a time until a soft dropping consistency is reached.

DIVIDE THE MIXTURE INTO TWO BOWLS and add the lemon zest to one bowl, stirring it in well. Mix the cocoa powder with a little water to form a paste, and add this paste to the other bowl of mixture, again stirring in well.

PUT ALTERNATE SPOONFULS OF EACH MIXTURE into the greased basin to give a marbled effect. Cover with a lid or a double layer of foil and steam for 1½–2 hours. Serve hot with chocolate sauce or custard.

Variation

For a more colourful pudding, the plain mixture can be tinted with a few drops of pink or red food colouring and flavoured with almond essence instead of lemon zest.

CHOCOHOLICS & NUTCASES

Chocolate bread and butter pudding

SERVES 4–6

12 slices of white bread
120–180g (4–6½oz)
  unsalted butter, softened,
  plus extra for greasing
Finely grated zest and juice
  of 1 orange
300g (11oz) dark chocolate,
  55–70% cocoa solids
3 eggs
600ml (1 pint) milk
90g (3oz) caster sugar
Cocoa powder, to dust
Custard, to serve

GREASE A 1.1-LITRE (2-pint) ovenproof baking dish. Remove the crusts from the bread and butter the slices on one side. Line the bottom and sides of the dish with some of the bread, butter-side up, and sprinkle with half the orange juice and zest.

BREAK THE CHOCOLATE INTO SMALL PIECES and sprinkle half of it across the bread, then cover with another layer of bread (again butter-side up), the remaining chocolate, juice and zest and finally the rest of the bread.

BEAT THE EGGS WELL and mix with the milk and sugar; pour this mixture over the bread. Leave to soak for 30 minutes, then preheat the oven to 200°C (400°F), Gas Mark 6 and bake for 30 minutes or until set. Dust with cocoa powder and serve hot with custard.

Hot mocha pudding

SERVES 4–6

110g (4oz) unsalted butter,
  softened, plus extra
  for greasing
50g (2oz) dark brown sugar
2 eggs
75g (3oz) self-raising flour
1 tbsp cocoa powder
Cream, to serve

For the mocha sauce
180g (6½oz) dark
  muscovado sugar
2 tbsp cocoa powder
225ml (8fl oz) milk
4 tbsp Tia Maria

PREHEAT THE OVEN TO 180°C (350°F), Gas Mark 4 and grease a 1.1-litre (2-pint) ovenproof baking dish. In a mixing bowl, beat together the butter, sugar, eggs, flour and cocoa powder until light and fluffy. Spoon the mixture into the greased dish.

COMBINE THE SUGAR AND COCOA POWDER for the sauce and sprinkle over the top of the mixture in the dish. Mix the milk and Tia Maria together and pour this over the top of the cocoa and sugar: do not stir in. Bake for approximately 1 hour until the sponge is cooked through. Serve with cream.

A recent addition to the English language, the word 'mocha' describes any combination of chocolate and coffee. It derives from the town of Mocha, in Yemen, which was a major trading centre for coffee beans between the 15th and 17th centuries. Mocha beans are still available today and prized for their distinctive flavour.

White chocolate and raspberry trifle

SERVES 6–8

2 Swiss rolls (store-bought or see page 92)

650g (1lb 7oz) raspberries

1 tbsp kirsch

450g (1lb) mascarpone cheese

300ml (11fl oz) double cream

200g (7oz) white chocolate

CUT THE SWISS ROLLS INTO SLICES about 1cm (½in) thick. Use these to line the bottom and sides of a large glass serving dish.

PUT THE RASPBERRIES IN A BOWL and pour the kirsch over them. With a spoon, lightly press the fruit to extract some juice. Spoon half of the raspberries and all of the juice and kirsch over the Swiss roll in the dish. Put in the fridge for 30 minutes until the juices are soaked up.

MEANWHILE, COMBINE THE MASCARPONE and cream in a mixing bowl and beat until completely combined. Break three quarters of the chocolate into small pieces and place in a small heatproof bowl over a saucepan of simmering water, ensuring the bowl doesn't touch the water. Stir until the chocolate is just melted and smooth.

SPOON HALF OF THE MELTED CHOCOLATE over the raspberries and Swiss roll in the dish and mix the other half with the mascarpone and cream. Add the mascarpone cream and remaining raspberries to the trifle in layers, finishing with a top layer of the cream. Grate the remaining chocolate over the top. Refrigerate for 30 minutes before serving.

Chocolate mousse

SERVES 6-8

225g (8oz) dark chocolate, 70% cocoa solids
25g (1oz) unsalted butter
4 eggs, separated
Few drops of vanilla essence
2–3 tsp orange liqueur
Whipped cream, to decorate
Fresh berries and mint leaves, or toasted almonds, to decorate

PUT THE CHOCOLATE AND BUTTER in a heatproof bowl set over a saucepan of simmering water. Leave to melt, stirring occasionally. Once the mixture has melted, remove the bowl from the heat and stir in the egg yolks, vanilla essence and liqueur.

IN A CLEAN BOWL, beat the egg whites until stiff but not dry. Gently fold the beaten whites into the melted chocolate in three or four batches, using a metal spoon. Divide the mousse among serving glasses or spoon into a large serving bowl and decorate with a little whipped cream. Arrange some berries and mint leaves on top, or scatter with toasted almonds.

It's helpful to beat in a spoonful of beaten egg white into the mixture before folding in the rest. This loosens the mixture and makes the folding easier.

Dark chocolate pavé

SERVES 12

1.5 litres (2½ pints) double cream

350g (12oz) dark chocolate, 55–70% cocoa solids

3 gelatine leaves

Soft red berries and/or mint leaves, to decorate

LINE A 1.5-LITRE (2½-pint) terrine mould with cling film. Set aside 150ml (5fl oz) of the double cream. Whip the rest of the cream to soft peaks.

MELT THE CHOCOLATE in a heatproof bowl set over a saucepan of simmering water, ensuring that the bottom of the bowl doesn't touch the water. Meanwhile, soak the gelatine leaves in cold water until soft. Remove from the water and put in a small saucepan with the reserved cream. Heat gently until the gelatine has dissolved.

FOLD THE WHIPPED CREAM into the melted chocolate, then add the warm cream and gelatine mixture, folding it in gently. Pour the mixture into the lined mould and refrigerate for 2 hours or until set. To serve, turn out of the mould onto a board or cold plate. Slice and decorate with the berries and/or mint leaves.

CHOCOHOLICS & NUTCASES

Pecan, cinnamon and maple syrup pudding

SERVES 6

50g (2oz) unsalted butter, softened, plus extra for greasing
75g (3oz) soft dark brown sugar
1 tbsp maple syrup
1 egg, beaten
100g (3½oz) self-raising flour
1 tsp ground cinnamon
3 tbsp milk, if required
50g (2oz) pecan nuts, chopped
Custard or cream, to serve

For the maple sauce
25g (1oz) unsalted butter
5 tsp double cream
40g (1½oz) maple syrup

GREASE A 1.1-LITRE (2-pint) pudding basin. To make the maple sauce, put the butter, double cream and maple syrup in a saucepan. Mix over a low heat until combined, then bring to the boil and simmer for 2 minutes. Pour the sauce into the bottom of the greased basin.

IN A MIXING BOWL, cream together the butter and sugar until pale and fluffy, then add the maple syrup. Gradually add the beaten egg, just a little at a time, then fold in the flour and cinnamon. If necessary, add milk until the mixture reaches a dropping consistency. Finally, stir in the chopped pecan nuts.

SPOON THE MIXTURE on top of the sauce in the pudding basin. Seal with a lid or foil and steam for 1½ hours. Turn out and serve with custard or cream.

Walnut and apple sponge pudding

SERVES 6

175ml (6fl oz) milk

2 tsp vanilla essence

2 tbsp cornflour

3 eggs

200g (7oz) soft light brown sugar

5 tbsp brandy

3 eating apples, peeled, cored and sliced

75g (3oz) shelled walnuts, chopped

75g (3oz) unsalted butter, plus extra for greasing

125g (4½oz) plain flour

1½ tsp baking powder

Whipped cream or Greek yoghurt, to serve

COMBINE THE MILK, vanilla essence, cornflour, one egg and 50g (2oz) of the sugar in a saucepan and whisk over a gentle heat until the mixture thickens into custard. Pour into a bowl and set aside to cool.

PUT 50g (2oz) of the sugar into a frying pan, along with the brandy and 5 tablespoons of water. Add the apples and walnuts and cook over a high heat until the liquid evaporates. Set aside to cool.

PREHEAT THE OVEN TO 180°C (350°F), Gas Mark 4 and grease a deep, 1.5-litre (2½-pint), ovenproof baking dish. In a mixing bowl, beat the remaining 100g (3½oz) of sugar with the butter until pale and fluffy, then add the two remaining eggs and mix to incorporate. Add the flour and baking powder and mix well.

CHOP UP THE SET CUSTARD and fold into the sponge mixture, then pour into the greased dish and spread the apple and walnut mix over the top, pressing the fruit and nuts into the pudding mixture. Bake for 45–50 minutes, then serve warm, with whipped cream or Greek yoghurt.

CHOCOHOLICS & NUTCASES

Walnut and toffee tart

SERVES 6

375g (13 oz) shortcrust pastry (see page 10), chilled
250g (9oz) caster sugar
300ml (11fl oz) whipping cream
180g (6½oz) walnuts
Ice cream or whipped cream, to serve

ROLL OUT THE CHILLED PASTRY on a floured surface, to 5mm (¼in) thickness, and use it to line a 30cm (12in) tart dish (see page 11). Refrigerate the lined dish for 30 minutes, then preheat the oven to 190°C (400°F), Gas Mark 5 and blind bake the pastry case for 25 minutes (see page 11).

WHILE THE PASTRY IS COOKING, put the sugar and cream in a saucepan and heat gently until the sugar has dissolved. Bring to the boil and remove immediately from the heat. Stir in the walnuts.

REMOVE THE PASTRY CASE FROM THE OVEN, and turn down the temperature to 190°C (375°F), Gas Mark 5. Pour the walnut filling into the cooked case, return to the oven and bake for a further 35 minutes. Remove from the oven and leave to cool, then refrigerate and serve cold with ice cream or whipped cream.

CHOCOHOLICS & NUTCASES

Maple, walnut and banana pudding

SERVES 4–6

Butter, for greasing
70g (2½oz) chopped
   walnuts
110ml (4fl oz) maple syrup
2 medium or 1 large ripe
   banana(s)
175g (6oz) self-raising flour
75g (3oz) vegetable suet
90g (3oz) caster sugar
1 egg, beaten
70ml (2½fl oz) milk
Custard, to serve

THOROUGHLY GREASE A 1.1-LITRE (2-pint) pudding basin and put half of the walnuts into the bottom with just enough of the maple syrup to cover them.

PEEL AND SLICE THE BANANA and mix with the flour, suet, sugar and remaining walnuts. Add the beaten egg, milk and remaining maple syrup and mix to a soft dropping consistency.

POUR THE MIXTURE OVER THE WALNUTS and syrup in the basin and cover with a lid or foil. Steam for 1½ hours, topping up the water as necessary. Serve with custard.

This unusual combination of flavours often causes consternation amongst Pudding Club guests, but it is wonderfully successful and they are always silenced after the first mouthful.

Date and walnut pudding

SERVES 6

Butter, for greasing
175g (6oz) self-raising flour
Pinch of salt
75g (3oz) shredded suet
50g (2oz) caster sugar
50g (2oz) chopped dates
50g (2oz) chopped walnuts
Grated zest of 1 unwaxed
   lemon
Approx. 150ml (5fl oz) milk
Custard or toffee sauce
   (see page 64), to serve

GREASE A 1.1 LITRE (2-pint) pudding basin.
In a mixing bowl, combine the flour, salt, suet,
sugar, dates, walnuts and lemon zest. Make a well
in the centre and add enough milk to reach a
dropping consistency.

POUR THE MIXTURE INTO THE GREASED BASIN
and smooth the surface. Cover the basin with a lid or
double layer of foil. Steam for 1½–2 hours, topping
up the water as necessary. Serve warm with custard
or with a little toffee sauce.

WHY NOT TRY...?
*While custard is the obvious option here, this
pudding is particularly delicious served with a
little sticky toffee sauce (see page 64).*

Hazelnut roulade

SERVES 6–8

4 egg whites

200g (7oz) caster sugar

1 tsp vanilla essence

1 tsp cornflour

1 tsp white wine or
    malt vinegar

3 gelatine leaves

375ml (13fl oz) double
    cream, plus extra to serve

100g (3½oz) praline
    paste/hazelnut purée
    (see tip below)

PREHEAT THE OVEN TO 160°C (325°F), Gas Mark 3. Whisk the egg whites in a large, scrupulously clean bowl until they form soft peaks, then gradually add the sugar, continuing to whisk as you do so. Add the vanilla essence, cornflour and vinegar and whisk until the mixture is stiff.

LINE A BAKING TRAY with non-stick baking parchment and spread the meringue mix evenly into a square of approximately 25cm (10in). Cook in the oven for 25 minutes, then remove from the oven and allow to cool before carefully removing the soft meringue from the parchment.

SOAK THE GELATINE LEAVES in cold water until soft. Remove from the water, and put in a small saucepan with 125ml (4½fl oz) of the cream. Heat gently to dissolve the gelatine. Whip the remaining cream to soft peaks.

MIX THE TWO CREAMS TOGETHER and carefully fold in the praline paste. Refrigerate the mixture until it has begun to stiffen, then spread evenly over the meringue and carefully roll up like a Swiss roll. Slice and serve with a little cream.

CHOCOHOLICS & NUTCASES

If you're struggling to find the hazelnut or praline paste used in this recipe, look for a brand called Callebaut, which can be found in some delicatessens or bought online.

SUMMER PUDDINGS

CHAPTER 7

Perfect for warm, sunny days, this selection of gorgeous
recipes makes the most of fresh summer flavours, including
apricots, cherries, gooseberries, peaches and elderflowers.
Get that holiday feeling with a floating island, refresh your
guests with a smooth lemon posset, or try your hand at the
world-famous peach Melba. And there's certainly no
need to shun hot puddings at this time of year; this chapter
suggests lighter, sponge-based options and refreshingly
sharp fruit bakes that are delicious at the end of
a barbecue or al fresco supper.

Peach Melba

SERVES 6

3 tbsp caster sugar
6 ripe peaches
375g (13oz) raspberries
Good-quality vanilla
    ice cream, to serve

PLACE 600ml (1 pint) water in a saucepan, add the caster sugar and heat to a gentle simmer. Add the whole peaches to the pan and poach until tender, over a low heat, for 15–20 minutes. Remove the peaches from the liquid and leave to cool. Keep some of the poaching liquor to use later.

ONCE THE PEACHES ARE COOL, cut in half and remove the stones. You can also skin them, if you wish. Put the raspberries in a blender with 1–2 tablespoons of the poaching liquor and blitz to a purée. Push the purée through a sieve to remove the seeds.

TO SERVE, PLACE A SCOOP of vanilla ice cream into each small serving bowl, add two poached peach halves and spoon some raspberry purée over the top.

Variation

Try using fresh blackcurrants to make the purée, instead of raspberries. The blackcurrants will need to be cooked gently before you blend them.

This simple but delicious dessert was invented by the world-famous chef Escoffier, in honour of Australian soprano Dame Nellie Melba, when she visited the Savoy in the late 19th century. Ice cream was still an exotic new arri... ' in Britain at the time.

Baked peaches

15g (½oz) unsalted butter, softened, plus extra for greasing
1 tbsp caster sugar
1 egg yolk
50g (2oz) amaretti or ratafia biscuits, crumbled
4 large ripe peaches or nectarines
Cream or ice cream, to serve

PREHEAT THE OVEN TO 180°C (350°F), Gas Mark 4 and lightly grease an ovenproof baking dish. In a mixing bowl, cream together the butter and sugar until pale and fluffy. Add the egg yolk and stir in the crumbled biscuits.

IF YOU ARE USING PEACHES (no need if using nectarines), place them in a saucepan and cover with boiling water. Leave for 2–3 minutes, then drain the water and peel off the skins. Halve the peaches or nectarines and remove the stones. Enlarge the cavities by scooping out some of the flesh with a teaspoon and adding the pulp to the biscuit mixture.

PILE THE BISCUIT STUFFING into the peach halves and arrange in the baking dish. Bake in the oven for 20–30 minutes until the peaches are soft but still holding their shape. Serve warm with cream or ice cream.

Apricot and almond puddings

MAKES 8

100g (3½oz) unsalted
   butter, softened, plus
   extra for greasing
100g (3½oz) caster sugar
2 eggs
100g (3½oz) self-raising
   flour
1 tsp almond essence
50g (2oz) ground almonds
240g (8½oz) stoned, diced
   fresh apricots (or cooked
   dried apricots)
40ml (1½fl oz) golden syrup
Custard or ice cream,
   to serve

PREHEAT THE OVEN TO 180°C (350°F), Gas Mark 4 and grease eight 200ml (7fl oz) pudding basins. In a mixing bowl, cream together the butter and sugar until pale and fluffy. Add the eggs gradually — if the mixture separates, just stir in a little of the flour. Add the almond essence, then fold in the remaining flour and ground almonds.

PLACE 30g (1oz) of the apricots and about 1 teaspoon of the syrup in the bottom of each greased basin. Divide the sponge mixture evenly between the basins and cover with lids or foil. Bake for approximately 15 minutes, until firm to the touch and golden brown. Serve with custard or ice cream.

Apricot tansy

SERVES 4–6

50g (2oz) unsalted butter

450g (1lb) fresh, ripe apricots, stoned and quartered

75g (3oz) caster sugar, plus extra for serving

4 eggs, plus 2 yolks

2 tbsp double cream

75g (3oz) fine white breadcrumbs

Pinch of ground nutmeg

Cream, to serve

MELT 35g (1½oz) of the butter in a heavy-based frying pan over a gentle heat. Add the apricots and sprinkle with 50g (2oz) of the sugar. Cook gently until softened but not coloured.

BEAT TOGETHER THE WHOLE EGGS, egg yolks, cream, breadcrumbs, nutmeg and the remaining 25g (1oz) of sugar. Pour this over the apricots in the pan, stirring together into one thick layer. Cook gently until golden brown underneath. Turn out onto a plate.

MELT THE REMAINING BUTTER in the pan and carefully slide the tansy back into the pan to cook the other side until golden brown. Turn out onto a warm plate and sprinkle with the extra sugar. Serve with cream.

Not unlike a sweet omelette, a tansy would once have been flavoured with the bittersweet juice of the tansy plant, a herb that is these days all but forgotten.

Apricot Turnovers

SERVES 6

450g (1lb) fresh, ripe
apricots, stoned and
quartered
Juice of 1 lemon
¼ tsp ground cinnamon
75g (3oz) caster sugar
450g (1lb) puff pastry
Flour, for dusting
1 egg
Vanilla ice cream, to serve

PUT THE APRICOTS IN A SAUCEPAN with the lemon juice, cinnamon, 50g (2oz) of the sugar and 1 tablespoon of water. Heat gently until the fruit has softened, stirring occasionally, then remove from the heat and leave to cool to room temperature.

PREHEAT THE OVEN TO 180°C (350°F), Gas Mark 4. Roll out the puff pastry on a floured surface, and cut out six 15cm (6in) squares. Place 3 tablespoons of the fruit mixture into the centre of each square. Beat the egg with a little water, and brush some of the egg mixture onto the edges of the pastry. Fold the pastry over to form triangles and press firmly to seal.

BRUSH THE TOP OF THE TRIANGLES with more of the egg mixture and sprinkle with the remaining caster sugar. Bake for 20–25 minutes until golden brown. Serve with vanilla ice cream.

Apple and apricot layer pudding

SERVES 4–6

2 medium eating apples
160g (5½oz) golden syrup
90g (3oz) raisins
300g (11oz) chopped
    dried apricots
1 tsp mixed spice
Butter, for greasing
Custard, to serve

For the suet pastry
240g (8½oz) self-raising
    flour, sifted, plus extra
    for dusting
110g (4oz) vegetable suet
30g (1oz) caster sugar
160ml (5½fl oz) milk

TO MAKE THE SUET PASTRY, mix the ingredients in a large bowl and bring the dough together with your hands. Roll out on a floured surface and cut out four circles, graduating in size to fit a 1.1-litre (2-pint) pudding basin.

PEEL AND CORE THE APPLES and chop into small pieces. Warm the golden syrup in a small saucepan or the microwave, then mix with the apples, raisins, apricots and mixed spice.

GREASE THE BASIN and put the smallest pastry circle in the base. Top with a layer of the fruit mixture. Add the next circle of pastry and repeat the layers, until you finish with the largest circle of pastry. Cover securely with a lid or foil and steam for 1½ hours. Turn out and serve with custard.

Holiday pudding

SERVES 6

2 tbsp golden syrup

1 x 225g tin of pineapple rings, drained

60g (2oz) glacé cherries

120g (4oz) unsalted butter, softened, plus extra for greasing

120g (4oz) caster sugar

2 large eggs, beaten

90g (3oz) self-raising flour

Pinch of salt

60g (2oz) breadcrumbs

60g (2oz) raisins

30g (1oz) chopped mixed candied peel

30g (1oz) chopped walnuts

Custard, to serve

GREASE A 1.5-LITRE (2½-pint) pudding basin and line the base with a circle of greaseproof paper. Put the golden syrup into the basin and arrange one drained pineapple ring in the bottom with a cherry in the centre. Cut two rings in half and arrange these halves around the first ring. Put a cherry in each hole. Chop the remaining pineapple rings and glacé cherries.

IN A MIXING BOWL, cream together the butter and sugar until pale and fluffy, then add the beaten eggs. Sift the flour and salt into a separate bowl and add to the creamed mixture along with the breadcrumbs. Mix well to incorporate, then stir in all the raisins, peel and nuts.

PILE THE MIXTURE ON TOP of the arranged fruit. Cover securely with a lid or foil and steam for 2 hours. Turn out and serve with custard.

There's a bright and cheerful tropical treat waiting to be revealed when you turn this pudding out.

Plum and cinnamon cobbler

SERVES 6–8

700g (1½lb) plums
Grated zest and juice
   of 1 orange
75g (3oz) soft light
   brown sugar
1 cinnamon stick
75g (3oz) unsalted butter
175g (6oz) plain flour
2 tsp baking powder
Pinch of salt
1 tsp ground cinnamon
125ml (4½fl oz) milk
1 tbsp demerara sugar
Thick cream, to serve

HALVE THE PLUMS and discard the stones. Put in a large saucepan with the orange juice, soft brown sugar and cinnamon stick and slowly bring to the boil. Simmer for 3–4 minutes, covered, then remove from the heat. Allow to cool in the pan for 45–60 minutes before pouring into a 23cm (9in) ovenproof baking dish, approximately 6cm (2½in) in depth.

PREHEAT THE OVEN TO 220°C (425°F), Gas Mark 7. In a mixing bowl, rub the butter into the flour, baking powder and salt until it resembles fine breadcrumbs (or use a food processor). Add the ground cinnamon and orange zest and stir in the milk until you a have a sticky, dough-like mixture.

SPOON THE MIXTURE OVER THE FRUIT in dollops and sprinkle generously with the demerara sugar. Bake in the oven for 25–30 minutes or until golden. The cobbler is best served warm with thick cream.

Steamed plum sponge

SERVES 4–6

1kg (2lb 2oz) fresh plums
230g (10oz) caster sugar
170g (6oz) unsalted butter,
  softened, plus extra
  for greasing
3 eggs, beaten
170g (6oz) self-raising
  flour, sifted
50ml (2fl oz) plum brandy
  or slivovitz
Custard, to serve

LIGHTLY GREASE A 1.1-LITRE (2-pint) pudding basin. Stone and quarter the plums and place in a medium saucepan with 60g (2oz) of the sugar. Cook gently for about 5 minutes until the plums begin to soften. Remove from the heat and allow to cool a little.

IN A MIXING BOWL, cream together the butter and remaining sugar until pale and fluffy. Gradually beat in the eggs, then mix in the flour and plum brandy. Mix well to combine.

PUT THREE QUARTERS OF THE SOFTENED PLUMS in the bottom of the greased basin and pour the sponge mixture on top. Cover with a lid or foil and steam for 1½ hours. Serve with custard and the remaining plums, reheated carefully so that they do not overcook.

SUMMER PUDDINGS

Blackcurrant and lemon sponge pudding

SERVES 6

100g (3½oz) good-quality
   blackcurrant jam,
   plus extra to serve
200g (7oz) unsalted butter,
   softened, plus extra
   for greasing
200g (7oz) golden caster
   sugar
3 large eggs, beaten
200g (7oz) self-raising flour
Grated zest of ½ unwaxed
   lemon
Cream or custard, to serve

GREASE A 1.1-LITRE (2-pint) pudding basin and place the blackcurrant jam in the base. In a mixing bowl, cream together the butter and sugar until pale and fluffy. Gradually add the beaten egg — if the mixture separates, just stir in a little of the flour.

FOLD IN THE REMAINING FLOUR and the lemon zest and spoon the sponge mixture over the jam in the greased basin. Cover with a lid or foil and steam for 2 hours. Once cooked, turn out onto a plate and serve with cream or custard, plus extra jam if you wish.

Gooseberry and almond pudding

SERVES 4

250g (9oz) gooseberries
  (fresh or frozen),
  topped and tailed
110g (4oz) caster sugar
60g (2oz) unsalted
  butter, softened
1 egg
30g (1oz) self-raising flour
30g (1oz) ground almonds
Custard, to serve

PREHEAT THE OVEN TO 170°C (325°F), Gas Mark 3. Put the gooseberries in an ovenproof baking dish and sprinkle with 50g (2oz) of the sugar.

IN A MIXING BOWL, cream together the butter and remaining 60g (2oz) of sugar until pale and fluffy. Beat in the egg. Sift the flour and fold this into the mixture, along with the ground almonds. Cover the gooseberries with this mixture.

BAKE THE PUDDING IN THE OVEN FOR 40–50 minutes until the sponge is golden brown and has risen. Serve with custard.

*If you use frozen gooseberries,
defrost first and drain off the
excess liquid.*

Gooseberry and orange pudding

SERVES 6

900g (2lb) gooseberries
(fresh or frozen),
topped and tailed

2 tbsp dark muscovado
sugar

Finely grated zest of 1
orange

Few drops of vanilla essence

175g (6oz) unsalted butter,
softened, plus extra
for greasing

175g (6oz) golden
caster sugar

3 large eggs

175g (6oz) self-raising flour

Custard, to serve

PREHEAT THE OVEN TO 200°C (400°F), Gas Mark 6 and grease a medium-sized ovenproof baking dish. Put the gooseberries into the dish and sprinkle with the muscovado sugar, orange zest and vanilla essence.

IN A MIXING BOWL, cream together the butter and caster sugar until pale and fluffy, then beat in the eggs. Sift in the flour and stir until incorporated. Spread the mixture over the gooseberries and bake for 40–50 minutes until the sponge has browned. If it looks like the pudding is browning too quickly, cover with foil. Serve with custard.

SUMMER PUDDINGS

179

Gooseberry and elderflower crumble

SERVES 8

650g (1lb 7oz) gooseberries (fresh or frozen), topped and tailed

250ml (9fl oz) elderflower cordial

Caster sugar, to taste

245g (8½oz) self-raising flour

165g (5½oz) demerara sugar

60g (2oz) margarine

60g (2oz) unsalted butter, cut into pieces

1 tsp vanilla essence

Custard or cream, to serve

PREHEAT THE OVEN TO 180°C (350°F), Gas Mark 4. Put the gooseberries in a large saucepan with the elderflower cordial and poach over a low heat for 10–15 minutes, until the fruit is lightly cooked but still holding its shape. Remove from the heat and add caster sugar to taste.

MEANWHILE, MAKE THE CRUMBLE TOPPING by sifting the flour into a large bowl and mixing in the demerara sugar. Add the margarine, butter and vanilla essence to the bowl and mix with your fingertips to the consistency of fine crumbs.

POUR THE GOOSEBERRIES and their poaching liquid into a deep, ovenproof baking dish, distribute the crumble mix on top and press down to firm. Cook in the oven for 45 minutes until golden brown. Serve with custard or cream.

This recipe combines two very traditional (and much underused) British ingredients to give a surprisingly modern twist on the classic fruit crumble. The result is wonderfully sweet and fragrant.

Gooseberry and elderflower layer pudding

SERVES 6–8

900g (2lb) green
   gooseberries (fresh or
   frozen), topped and tailed
3 elderflower heads
600g (1lb 5oz) caster sugar
50g (2oz) unsalted butter
12 slices of white bread,
   crusts removed
225ml (8fl oz) milk
450ml (16fl oz) double
   cream
4 large eggs, lightly beaten
1 tsp vanilla essence
15g (½oz) soft light
   brown sugar
Cream or crème fraîche,
   to serve

PUT THE GOOSEBERRIES, ELDERFLOWERS AND 450g (1lb) of the caster sugar in a medium saucepan and stir very gently over a medium heat until the gooseberries have split open. Remove the elderflowers and discard them.

BUTTER THE BREAD and arrange four slices, butter-side down, in a single layer in a 20cm (8in) square, ovenproof baking dish. Spread about a third of the gooseberry mixture over the bread, then top with another four pieces of bread, butter-side down. Add another third of the gooseberry mix, then top with the final four slices of bread, again butter-side down, to complete the layers. Keep the final third of the gooseberry mixture for serving.

IN A BOWL, WHISK TOGETHER the milk, cream, eggs, vanilla essence and remaining 150g (5oz) of caster sugar, then pour this over the top of the pudding. Sprinkle the brown sugar over the top, and allow the pudding to rest for an hour.

PREHEAT THE OVEN TO 180°C (350°F), Gas Mark 4. Place the baking dish in a large roasting tin and pour water into the tin to come halfway up the sides of the dish. Bake in the oven for 1 hour or until the top of the pudding is golden brown. Serve warm with the reserved gooseberry mixture and cream or crème fraîche.

Lemon posset

SERVES 6

550ml (19fl oz) double
or whipping cream
140g (5oz) caster sugar
Finely grated zest and juice
of 2 large unwaxed lemons
6 sponge finger biscuits

PUT THE CREAM AND SUGAR in a large saucepan and gradually bring to the boil. Simmer for 3 minutes then remove from the heat. Whisk in the lemon juice and zest until completely incorporated.

POUR THE MIXTURE INTO SIX SERVING GLASSES or ramekins and chill for about 2 hours. Gently dip the sponge finger biscuits into the posset just before serving.

Dating back to the 15th century, the posset began life as a drink made from milk and flavoured with spices, devised as a remedy for illness. It even appears in Shakespeare, when Lady Macbeth uses 'drugg'd' possets to poison the guards who block her way.

SUMMER PUDDINGS

Lemon layer pudding

SERVES 6

2 eggs

180g (6½oz) caster sugar

Finely grated zest and juice
of 2 unwaxed lemons

60g (2oz) unsalted butter,
melted, plus extra
for greasing

Custard, to serve

For the suet pastry

240g (8½oz) self-raising
flour, plus extra for
dusting

Pinch of salt

120g (4oz) vegetable suet

GREASE A 1.1-LITRE (2-pint) pudding basin.
To make the suet pastry, sift the flour and salt into
a large bowl and mix in the suet. Add enough cold
water to form a soft dough.

ROLL OUT HALF OF THE PASTRY on a floured
surface and use it to line the greased basin. Divide
the rest of the pastry roughly into two, and roll these
pieces out to make layers of pastry that graduate in
size for the middle and top of the pudding.

TO MAKE THE FILLING, beat together the eggs,
sugar, lemon zest and juice and melted butter.
Pour half of this mixture into the lined basin, add
the central layer of pastry, pour in the remaining
mixture and top with the final layer of pastry.
Cover securely with a lid or foil and steam for
2½–3 hours. Turn out and serve with custard.

Raspberry, apple and almond crumble

SERVES 8

245g (8½oz) self-raising flour

185g (6½oz) demerara sugar

60g (2oz) unsalted butter, cut into pieces

60g (2oz) margarine

60g (2oz) flaked or nibbed almonds

1 tsp almond essence

250g (9oz) raspberries

450g (1lb) peeled, cored and chopped cooking apple

Caster sugar, to taste

Custard or whipped vanilla cream (see box), to serve

PREHEAT THE OVEN TO 200°C (400°F), Gas Mark 6. Sift the flour into a large bowl and mix in the demerara sugar. Add the butter and margarine and mix with your fingertips to a fine crumb consistency. Add the almonds and almond essence and mix through.

MIX TOGETHER THE RASPBERRIES, apple and caster sugar and place in the base of a deep, 30cm (12in), ovenproof baking dish. Add the crumble topping and firm down a little. Bake in the oven for approximately 45 minutes until golden brown. Serve with custard or whipped vanilla cream.

WHY NOT TRY…?
This pudding is lovely served with vanilla-flavoured whipped cream. Simply add a little vanilla extract, or the seeds from a vanilla pod, to double or whipping cream and whip as normal.

SUMMER PUDDINGS

Blackberry charlotte

SERVES 6–8

110g (4oz) caster sugar,
  plus extra to taste
450g (1lb) blackberries
1½ tbsp cornflour
2 eggs, separated
4½ tbsp double or whipping
  cream, plus extra to serve
Juice of ½ lemon
110g (4oz) sponge finger
  biscuits
110g (4oz) icing sugar

PUT THE CASTER SUGAR and 275ml (½ pint) water in a pan and heat gently until the sugar has dissolved. Add the blackberries and cook over a low heat for 10 minutes. Strain and reserve the syrup, putting the blackberries to one side.

TO MAKE THE BLACKBERRY CREAM, put the cornflour in a small saucepan and gradually blend in 275ml (½ pint) of the syrup (reserve the remaining syrup to use in the meringue). Cook for a few minutes, stirring, then remove from the heat. Beat the egg yolks and cream into the cornflour mixture. Add the lemon juice and more sugar if required.

CUT OFF ONE ROUNDED END OF EACH sponge finger. Pour enough of the blackberry cream into a 570ml (1-pint) ovenproof glass or Pyrex soufflé dish to cover the bottom and stand the sponge fingers, cut-side down and sugar-side out, around the inside edge of the dish until completely lined. Arrange a layer of the reserved blackberries over the cream, followed by another layer of cream, repeating until the berries and cream are used up.

PREHEAT THE OVEN TO 150°C (300°F), Gas Mark 2. Put the egg whites, icing sugar and 4½ tablespoons of the blackberry syrup in a medium–large heatproof bowl set over a saucepan of simmering water. Whisk until the meringue reaches soft peaks. Remove the bowl from the heat and keep whisking until the meringue has cooled. Pile or pipe the meringue onto the top of the pudding and bake for 20 minutes. Leave to cool and serve cold with whipped cream.

SUMMER PUDDINGS

187

Lattice cherry pie

SERVES 4

250g (9oz) shortcrust
　pastry (see page 10)
500g (1lb 2oz) cherries
75g (3oz) caster sugar
1 tbsp cornflour
30g (1oz) unsalted butter,
　plus extra for greasing
Squeeze of lemon juice
1 egg, beaten
Pouring cream, to serve

PREHEAT THE OVEN TO 180°C (350°F), Gas Mark 4. Lightly grease a 20cm (8in) shallow pie dish. Roll out the chilled pastry on a floured surface, to 5mm (¼in) thickness, and line the pie dish (see page 11). Keep the pastry trimmings.

REMOVE THE STEMS AND STONES from the cherries. Put the fruit in a saucepan with the sugar, cornflour, butter, lemon juice and 1 tablespoon of water. Gently bring to the boil and cook for 1 minute. Remove from the heat and allow to cool slightly, then spoon into the uncooked pastry case.

MAKE A LATTICE TOP from the pastry trimmings. Brush the top with a little beaten egg and bake the pie in the oven for 30–40 minutes until the pastry is cooked and golden brown. Serve with pouring cream.

Floating island

SERVES 4

15g (½oz) unsalted butter
100g (4oz) sugared
 almonds, in mixed colours
4 eggs, separated
250g (9oz) caster sugar,
 plus extra for the tin
275ml (½ pint) milk
Few drops of vanilla essence

PREHEAT THE OVEN TO 175°C (350°C), Gas Mark 3–4. Use the butter to grease a deep, round, 15cm (6in) cake tin and coat it with a little sugar. Wrap the sugared almonds in a clean tea towel and crush them coarsely with a rolling pin.

IN A SCRUPULOUSLY CLEAN BOWL, whisk the egg whites until stiff, then gradually add 110g (4oz) of the sugar, continuing to whisk as you do so. Gently fold a further 110g (4oz) of the sugar into the egg whites with a metal spoon.

POUR ONE THIRD OF THIS MERINGUE MIXTURE into the prepared tin, followed by half the crushed almonds, a further third of the egg-white mixture, the rest of the almonds and finally a top layer of meringue. Place the cake tin in a roasting tin and pour boiling water around it to a depth of about 2.5cm (1in). Bake for 30 minutes then remove from the oven and leave to cool.

WHILE THIS IS COOKING, beat the eggs yolks with the remaining 30g (1oz) of sugar. Heat the milk in a small saucepan until almost boiling, then stir in the egg-yolk mixture. Blend thoroughly and strain into a heatproof bowl set over a saucepan of simmering water. Stir gently for about 10 minutes until you have thickening custard. Remove from the heat, add a few drops of vanilla essence and allow the custard to cool, stirring regularly to prevent a skin forming. Pour the cooled custard into a large, deep, round bowl. Carefully loosen the meringue from the tin with a small knife and place onto the custard. Serve cold.

WINTER PUDDINGS

As the weather grows colder and the nights draw in, what better way to warm your cockles than with a generous bowl of something steaming and sweet? In this chapter you'll find an array of hot, hearty puddings, along with ideas for using up the glut of pears, blackberries and other late-autumn fruits. There are also plenty of recipes for the festive season, giving you the choice of a traditional Christmas pud, a modern version that can be cooked entirely in the microwave, or the quick-to-make St Nick's pudding for those who prefer a lighter option. And instead of traditional mince pies, why not serve your guests our mincemeat tart or roly poly along with mulled wine jelly for a Christmas party with a difference?

Apple and mincemeat pudding

SERVES 4–6

1 tbsp brandy

140g (5oz) mincemeat

150g (5½oz) unsalted butter, softened, plus extra for greasing

125g (4½oz) caster sugar

3 eggs, beaten

170g (6oz) self-raising flour

1 tbsp baking powder

2 small eating apples

Custard, to serve

GREASE A 1.1-LITRE (2-pint) pudding basin. Stir the brandy into the mincemeat and place in the bottom of the greased basin. In a mixing bowl, cream together the butter and sugar until pale and fluffy, then gradually mix in the beaten eggs.

SIFT THE FLOUR AND BAKING POWDER together and fold into the creamed mixture. Core and roughly chop the apples into 1cm (½in) pieces and stir into the mixture. Pour the sponge mixture over the mincemeat in the basin, cover securely with a lid or foil and steam for 1½ hours. Serve with custard.

If you don't make your own mincemeat buy a ready-made version and add more brandy, cherry, almonds or whatever you fancy.

Bramley apple and lemon curd puddings

MAKES 6

115g (4oz) unsalted butter, softened, plus extra for greasing
115g (4oz) caster sugar
2 eggs
½ tsp vanilla essence
Grated unwaxed lemon zest, to taste
115g (4oz) self-raising flour
2 tbsp milk
Cream or custard, to serve

For the apple and lemon curd
225g (8oz) Bramley apples, peeled, cored and chopped
Grated zest of 1 unwaxed lemon
65g (2½oz) unsalted butter
125g (4½oz) granulated sugar
50ml (2fl oz) fresh lemon juice
2 eggs, beaten

FIRST MAKE THE APPLE AND LEMON CURD. Put the chopped apples in a saucepan with the lemon zest and 50ml (2fl oz) water. Cook until soft, then remove from the heat and push through a sieve or process in the pan with a hand blender until you have a smooth purée.

PUT THE APPLE PURÉE into a large heatproof bowl with the butter, sugar and lemon juice and set over a saucepan of simmering water. As soon as the butter has melted, press the beaten egg through a sieve into the bowl and whisk to combine. (If you have a cooking thermometer, make sure the mixture is not above 55°C when adding the egg, or it will scramble.) Stir over a gentle heat until the mixture is thick and creamy; this will take about 5–6 minutes. Leave to cool.

IN A MIXING BOWL, cream together the butter and caster sugar until pale and fluffy. Gradually add the eggs – if the mixture separates, just stir in a little of the flour. Add the vanilla essence and lemon zest. Fold in the remaining flour in stages, then add milk until a dropping consistency is achieved.

PREHEAT THE OVEN TO 180°C (350°F), Gas Mark 4 and grease six 200ml (7fl oz) ovenproof pudding basins. Place 40g (1½oz) of the cooled apple and lemon curd into each pudding basin. Divide the sponge mix evenly among the pudding moulds.

BAKE IN THE OVEN FOR approximately 15 minutes until firm to the touch and golden. Remove from the oven and turn out onto serving plates. Serve with cream or custard.

WINTER PUDDINGS

Apple and cinnamon amber

SERVES 4–6

450g (1lb) peeled, cored cooking apples
50g (2oz) unsalted butter, plus extra for greasing
200g (7oz) caster sugar
225g (8oz) fresh white bread
½ tsp ground cinnamon
3 eggs, separated

PREHEAT THE OVEN TO 180°C (350°F), Gas Mark 4 and grease a 20cm (8in) pie dish. Quarter the apples and cut each piece in half again. Put in a saucepan with the butter and 50g (2oz) of the sugar. Cook over a gentle heat until the fruit mixture is soft and thick.

PROCESS THE BREAD INTO FINE BREADCRUMBS and stir into the fruit mixture along with the cinnamon. Beat the egg yolks into the mixture, pour into the pie dish and bake in the oven for 30 minutes.

MEANWHILE, WHISK THE EGG WHITES in a scrupulously clean bowl until they form stiff peaks. Add half the remaining sugar and whisk until the mixture is thick and shiny. Fold in the remaining sugar with a metal spoon and pile the meringue onto the cooked fruit base. Return to the oven and bake for another 10 minutes, then serve immediately.

Elderberry, blackberry and apple pudding

SERVES 6–8

450g (1lb) cooking apples, peeled, cored and sliced

110g (4oz) blackberries

50g (2oz) elderberries, stalks removed

1 heaped tbsp seedless raspberry jam

175g (6oz) unsalted butter, softened, plus extra for greasing

150g (5oz) light brown muscovado sugar

1 tbsp golden syrup

4 eggs, beaten

110g (4oz) self-raising flour

110g (4oz) ground almonds

1 tsp baking powder

½ tsp almond extract

Cream or ice cream, to serve

THOROUGHLY GREASE A 1.1-LITRE (2-pint) ovenproof baking dish. Put the apples, blackberries, elderberries and jam into a saucepan, cover with a lid and cook gently for 10–15 minutes until soft. Pour into the baking dish.

PREHEAT THE OVEN TO 170°C (325°F), Gas Mark 3. In a mixing bowl, beat together the butter, sugar and golden syrup until pale, then gradually add the eggs, beating well between each addition. Fold in the flour, ground almonds, baking powder and almond extract. Pour onto the fruit mixture in the baking dish. Smooth the top and bake in the oven for 30–40 minutes until the sponge is golden brown and firm to the touch. If it looks like it is browning too quickly during cooking, cover with foil. Serve with cream or ice cream.

Autumn pear pudding

SERVES 4–6

Butter, for greasing
120g (4oz) self-raising flour
Pinch of salt
120g (4oz) breadcrumbs
120g (4oz) vegetable suet
120g (4oz) sultanas
90g (3oz) caster sugar
1 egg, beaten
120g (4oz) golden syrup
Finely grated zest and juice
   of ½ orange
1 large pear, peeled, cored
   and chopped or grated
Custard, to serve

GREASE A 1.1-LITRE (2-pint) pudding basin. Sift the flour and salt together into a large bowl and mix in the breadcrumbs, suet, sultanas and sugar.

BLEND THE BEATEN EGG with the golden syrup, orange juice and zest, then mix into the dry mixture along with the chopped or grated pear. Stir well and pour into the pudding basin. Cover securely with a lid or foil and steam for 3 hours. Turn out and serve with custard.

Pear and ginger upside-down pudding

SERVES 6

165g (5½oz) unsalted butter, plus extra for greasing

140g (5oz) soft dark brown sugar

3 pears, peeled, cored and quartered

30g (1oz) stem ginger, chopped

115g (4oz) black treacle

115g (4oz) golden syrup

2 tsp ground cinnamon

2 tsp ground ginger

¼ tsp ground nutmeg

2 eggs, beaten

150ml (5fl oz) milk

225g (8oz) plain flour, sifted

1 tsp baking powder

Custard or ice cream, to serve

PREHEAT THE OVEN TO 180°C (350°F), Gas Mark 4. Grease a deep, round, 23cm (9in) cake tin and line with greaseproof paper. Put 50g (2oz) of the butter and 70g (2½oz) of the sugar in a saucepan and heat gently until the sugar has dissolved. Pour into the base of the lined tin, arrange the quartered pears on top and sprinkle with the chopped stem ginger.

PLACE THE REMAINING BUTTER AND SUGAR in a saucepan with the treacle and golden syrup. Heat gently until combined, then remove from the heat and add the cinnamon, ginger and nutmeg, followed by the beaten egg and the milk. Finally add the sifted flour and baking powder and mix to form a smooth batter.

POUR THE BATTER OVER THE PEARS in the tin and bake in the oven for 40–50 minutes. Check with a skewer that the pudding is cooked through, then turn out onto a serving plate and serve with custard or ice cream.

WINTER PUDDINGS

Pears poached in mulled wine

SERVES 8

600ml (1 pint) full-bodied
   red wine
Grated zest and juice
   of 1 orange
4 cloves
1 cinnamon stick
Small piece of fresh root
   ginger, peeled and sliced
1 vanilla pod, split
   lengthways
300g (11oz) caster sugar
8 slightly under-ripe pears
   (Conference are ideal)
Ice cream, to serve

FIRST YOU NEED TO MULL THE WINE. Place
all the ingredients, except for the pears, in a large
saucepan, add 600ml (1 pint) water and bring
to the boil, then reduce the heat and simmer for
5 minutes.

PEEL THE PEARS, lower into the simmering wine
syrup and weigh them down with a plate so that they
are fully submerged. Cover the pan with a lid. Check
the pears after 20 minutes — they should offer no
resistance when pricked with a sharp knife. Continue
to cook if necessary. Once cooked, remove from the
heat and leave the pears to cool in the syrup. Serve
with ice cream.

Raisin ginger pudding

SERVES 4–6

Butter, for greasing
120g (4oz) plain flour
½ tsp bicarbonate of soda
Pinch of salt
120g (4oz) breadcrumbs
1 tsp ground ginger
1 tsp ground allspice
90g (3oz) vegetable suet
90g (3oz) raisins
20g (¾oz) stem ginger, chopped
60g (2oz) golden syrup
Milk, to mix
Custard, to serve

GREASE A 1.1-LITRE (2-pint) pudding basin. Sift the flour, bicarbonate of soda and salt together into a large bowl, then mix in all the remaining dry ingredients, including the raisins and stem ginger.

MELT THE GOLDEN SYRUP in a small saucepan or the microwave, add to the mixed dry ingredients and stir in enough milk to reach a dropping consistency. Spoon into the basin, cover securely with a lid or foil and steam for 3 hours. Turn out and serve with custard.

Soak the raisins in ginger wine for an hour or two before using. Have a tipple yourself too, but not so many that you tip over!

Seville orange marmalade bread and butter pudding

SERVES 4–6

120–180g (4–6½oz)
  unsalted butter, softened,
  plus extra for greasing
12 slices of white bread,
  crusts removed
200g (7oz) medium-cut
  Seville orange marmalade
3 eggs
600ml (1 pint) milk
90g (3oz) caster sugar
Ground cinnamon or
  nutmeg, to sprinkle
Custard, to serve (optional)

GREASE A 1.1-litre (2-pint) ovenproof baking dish.

BUTTER THE BREAD SLICES on one side. Line the bottom and sides of the greased dish with some of the bread, butter-side up. If there any large pieces of rind in the marmalade, cut them into smaller 2cm (¾in) pieces, then spread half of the marmalade over the bread. Add another layer of bread and spread the rest of the marmalade onto this layer. Finish with the remaining bread.

BEAT THE EGGS WELL, mix with the milk and sugar, and pour this mixture over the pudding. Sprinkle with cinnamon or nutmeg and leave to soak for 30 minutes, then preheat the oven to 200°C (400°F), Gas Mark 6 and bake the pudding for 30 minutes or until set. Serve hot, on its own or with custard.

Blood orange puddings

4 blood oranges

120g (4oz) butter, softened, plus extra for greasing

120g (4oz) caster sugar, plus an extra 3 tbsp for the syrup

120g (4oz) self-raising flour, sifted

2 eggs, beaten

1 tbsp golden syrup

Custard or ice cream, to serve

FINELY GRATE THE ZEST OF two of the blood oranges, then peel and segment them and set the segments aside. In a mixing bowl, cream the butter and sugar until pale and fluffy, then add the orange zest. Add the sifted flour to the creamed mixture a little at a time, alternating with the beaten egg, and beating well after each addition.

GREASE FOUR 200ml (7fl oz) pudding basins. Put a little of the golden syrup into the bottom of each basin. Place a couple of the reserved orange segments in the base of each basin (keep the remaining segments to one side). Divide the sponge mixture equally between the basins. Cover securely with lids or foil and steam for 30 minutes.

WHILE THE PUDDINGS ARE COOKING, juice the remaining two oranges, place the juice and the reserved orange segments into a small pan with the caster sugar. Heat over a medium heat to reduce the liquid and make an orange syrup.

TURN OUT THE PUDDINGS and top with the orange segments and syrup. Serve with custard or ice cream.

Tarter than regular oranges and with glorious red flesh, blood oranges mostly come from southern Mediterranean countries. In season from December to March, they bring a hint of sunshine to our cold winter months.

SERVES 4–6

Figgy pudding

Butter, for greasing
120g (4oz) plain flour
Pinch of salt
120g (4oz) breadcrumbs
120g (4oz) vegetable suet
1 tsp mixed spice
1 tsp baking powder
90g (3oz) dark soft
  brown sugar
240g (8½oz) figs, chopped
Finely grated zest of
  1 unwaxed lemon
2 tbsp milk
2 eggs, beaten
Warmed golden syrup and
  custard, to serve

GREASE A 1.1-LITRE (2-pint) pudding basin. Sift the flour and salt together into a large bowl, then add all the remaining dry ingredients and mix to combine. Add the figs, lemon zest and juice, milk and eggs, then beat well. The mixture should reach a soft dropping consistency.

POUR THE MIXTURE into the greased basin, cover securely with a lid or foil and steam for 3 hours. Serve with warmed golden syrup and custard.

WINTER PUDDINGS

A modern Christmas pudding

SERVES 10

Butter, for greasing

90g (3oz) plain flour

¼ tsp salt

90g (3oz) vegetable suet

½ tsp mixed spice

¼ tsp ground cinnamon

45g (1½oz) breadcrumbs

60g (2oz) caster sugar

60g (2oz) chopped mixed
 candied peel

60g (2oz) dark soft
 brown sugar

60g (2oz) glacé cherries,
 chopped

90g (3oz) currants

90g (3oz) raisins

120g (4oz) sultanas

45g (1½oz) blanched
 almonds, chopped

30g (1oz) peeled, cored and
 chopped cooking apple

Juice and finely grated zest
 of ½ unwaxed lemon

2 tsp golden syrup

2 tsp gravy browning

4 tbsp brandy

2 eggs, beaten

4 tbsp milk

Brandy butter or rich white
 brandy sauce, to serve

GREASE A 1.7-LITRE (3-pint) pudding basin. Sift the flour and salt together into a large mixing bowl, then add all the dry ingredients on the list, down to and including the apple and lemon zest and mix until combined. Stir in all the remaining ingredients and pour the pudding mixture into the greased basin.

COVER SECURELY WITH A LID or double layer of greaseproof paper. Cook in an 800W (or above) microwave on the High setting for 5 minutes, leave to stand for 5 minutes, then repeat. Serve straight away or store in the fridge until needed and reheat as described below. Serve with brandy butter or a rich white brandy sauce.

TO REHEAT, REMOVE THE PUDDING from the basin and sprinkle with 1½ teaspoons of water. Cover with cling film and cook in the microwave for 4 minutes. Leave for 4 minutes, then cook for a further 3 minutes.

We devised this 'modern' Christmas pudding specifically so that it can be cooked in your microwave. (Don't have a microwave? Turn to page 214 for the traditional version.)

WINTER PUDDINGS

Old Hooky Christmas pudding

SERVES 8–12

1.2kg (2½lb) mixed
  dried fruit
240g (8½oz) ready-soaked
  prunes, chopped
240g (8½oz) breadcrumbs
2 large cooking apples,
  peeled and grated
60g (2oz) blanched
  almonds, chopped
1 tsp mixed spice
Finely grated zest and
  juice of 1 unwaxed lemon
  and 1 orange
240g (8½oz) soft dark
  brown sugar
120g (4oz) glacé cherries
1 large carrot, peeled and
  grated
120g (4oz) ground almonds
120g (4oz) plain flour
½ tsp ground cinnamon
½ tsp ground nutmeg
240g (8½oz) shredded
  vegetable suet
1 tsp salt
150–200ml (5–7fl oz) Old
  Hooky or similar dark ale
1 small glass of brandy
  (about 50ml/2fl oz)
3 eggs, beaten
Butter, for greasing
Brandy butter, to serve

MIX TOGETHER ALL THE INGREDIENTS in a large mixing bowl, give them a good stir and leave to stand, covered, overnight.

THE FOLLOWING DAY, grease two 1.1-litre (2-pint) pudding basins and pour in the mixture, filling the basins right to the top. Cover securely with lids or foil and steam for 1–1½ hours. Serve with brandy butter.

Fans of real ale will love this festive pudding. Old Hooky is a fruity, full-bodied beer brewed in the Oxfordshire village of Hook Norton. Of course other dark ales can be used instead, but you'll have to rename your pudding accordingly!

Plum duff

SERVES 4–6

150g (5oz) self-raising flour,
plus extra for sprinkling
75g (3oz) shredded suet
100g (3½oz) currants
100g (3½oz) raisins
100g (3½oz) demerara
sugar
Pinch of mixed spice
Approx. 150ml (5fl oz) milk
Custard or melted jam,
to serve

IN A LARGE BOWL, mix together the flour, suet, currants, raisins, sugar and spice. Mix with enough milk to form a stiff dough. Soak a clean tea towel or pudding cloth in boiling water, wring then open out flat and sprinkle with a little flour. Put the dough into the centre of the floured cloth and tie up like a football.

DROP THE WRAPPED DOUGH into a saucepan of boiling water, cover and boil for 1½ hours, adding more water to the pan as necessary so that it doesn't boil dry. At the end of the cooking time, remove the pudding from the pan and unwrap carefully. Serve with custard or melted jam.

Originally known as 'plum dough', this began life as a British 'street food', sold from cloth–covered baskets by street vendors' wives. These days, people often wonder why plum duff contains no plums, but back in the 17th century, the word was used to refer to all manner of fruits, including raisins and currants.

WINTER PUDDINGS

St Nick's puddings

MAKES 6

170g (6oz) unsalted
  butter, softened, plus
  extra for greasing
170g (6oz) soft light
  brown sugar
3 eggs, beaten
125g (4½oz) self-raising
  flour
140g (5oz) white
  breadcrumbs
1 tsp ground cinnamon
Grated zest of 1 orange
  and juice of ½
40g (1½oz) chopped prunes
190g (6½oz) chopped plums
3 tbsp golden syrup
Custard, to serve

GREASE SIX 200ml (7FL OZ) PUDDING BASINS. In a mixing bowl, cream together the butter and sugar until pale and fluffy. Gradually add the beaten egg and stir to combine — if the mixture separates, just stir in a little of the flour. Fold in the remaining flour, breadcrumbs and cinnamon and mix well. Add the orange zest, juice, prunes and 100g (3½oz) of the plums.

PLACE 15g (½oz) OF THE REMAINING PLUMS with ½ tablespoon of the golden syrup in the base of each greased basin. Divide the sponge mix evenly among them and seal with lids or foil. Steam for 35–45 minutes until cooked, then turn out and serve with custard.

A nice change from the usual Christmas pud, this lighter alternative is also much quicker to make as — unlike the traditional recipe — it doesn't need to be left for weeks to mature. Definitely one for those who've left their Christmas preparations until the last minute!

Christmas pudding

SERVES 12

1.2kg (2½lb) mixed
  dried fruits
240g (8½oz) ready-soaked
  prunes, chopped
240g (8½oz) breadcrumbs
2 large cooking apples,
  peeled, chopped and
  grated
60g (2oz) blanched
  almonds, chopped
1 tsp mixed spice
Finely grated zest and juice
  of 1 unwaxed lemon
  and 1 orange
240g (8½oz) soft dark
  brown sugar
120g (4oz) glacé cherries
1 large carrot, peeled
  and grated
120g (4oz) ground almonds
120g (4oz) plain flour
½ tsp ground cinnamon
½ tsp ground nutmeg
240g (8½oz) vegetable suet
1 tsp salt
220ml (8fl oz) stout
  (½ regular can)
50ml (2fl oz) brandy
3 eggs, beaten
Butter, for greasing

MIX TOGETHER ALL THE INGREDIENTS in a large bowl, stir well to combine, cover the bowl and leave to stand overnight.

THE FOLLOWING DAY, grease two 1.1-litre (2-pint) pudding basins or one 2.3-litre (4-pint) basin. Pour the mixture into the greased basin(s), right up to the top. Cover securely with a lid or foil and steam the smaller puddings for 6 hours or the larger one for 10 hours. Serve with your choice of accompaniments (see below).

WHY NOT TRY...?
Christmas pudding takes a long time to cook, so make your celebrations less stressful by cooking it in advance and simply reheating when needed. To reheat, steam the smaller puddings for about 1 hour; the larger for 2 hours. Douse in rum or brandy, set alight if you wish, and serve with your choice of brandy butter, white sauce, custard or cream.

Mincemeat roly poly

SERVES 4–6

180g (6½oz) self-raising
  flour, plus extra for
  dusting
Pinch of salt
90g (3oz) vegetable suet
Finely grated zest
  of 1 unwaxed lemon
Milk, to mix
450g (1lb) mincemeat
1 tbsp caster sugar
Custard, to serve

PREHEAT THE OVEN TO 190°C (375°F), Gas Mark 5. Sift the flour and salt together into a large bowl, then add the suet, lemon zest and enough milk to make a dough. On a floured surface, roll out the dough to about 25cm (10in) square and spread with the mincemeat. Dampen the edges of the dough with water and roll up like a Swiss roll.

PLACE THE ROLY POLY IN A ROASTING TIN and put in the oven, raising one side of the tin so that the pudding rolls to one end. This will prevent it from unravelling. Bake for 1 hour. (Alternatively, wrap the pudding in foil to hold its shape and in cling film to make it watertight. Steam for 1½ hours, then carefully remove the cling film and foil.) Sprinkle with the sugar and serve with custard.

WINTER PUDDINGS

Mulled wine jelly

SERVES 6

1 orange

1 unwaxed lemon

2 slices of fresh root ginger, peeled

1 small cinnamon stick

2 cloves

200ml (7fl oz) port

1 bottle of fruity red wine

150g (5oz) granulated sugar

25g (1oz) gelatine leaves

Crème fraîche, to serve

FINELY PARE THE ZEST from the orange and lemon and place the strips in a bowl with the ginger, cinnamon and cloves. Squeeze in the orange and lemon juice, cover and leave to macerate overnight.

THE NEXT DAY, pour the mixture into a large, stainless-steel saucepan and add the port, wine and sugar. Heat gently, stirring occasionally, until the sugar has dissolved. The mixture should never reach a simmer. As soon as it is piping hot, remove from the heat.

PLACE THE GELATINE IN A LARGE BOWL. Keep the leaves loose and slightly separate from each other as you pour on enough cold water to cover them. Leave to soak for 5 minutes, then drain off the water. Strain the hot wine through a fine sieve onto the soft gelatine and stir until the gelatine has dissolved. Leave to cool.

POUR THE COOLED JELLY MIXTURE into a large glass dish or individual glasses. Chill in the fridge overnight until set, then serve with crème fraîche, flavoured if you wish (see below).

After a Christmas party one year, Jill from The Pudding Club was left wondering what to do with a surplus of mulled wine. She decided to try making it into a jelly and was very pleasantly surprised by the results!

WHY NOT TRY...?

This jelly is divine served with crème fraîche, which can be flavoured with calvados, orange blossom water or Cointreau for a refreshing fruity kick.

WINTER PUDDINGS

Mincemeat tart

SERVES 8–10

375g (13oz) shortcrust pastry (see page 10)

Flour, for dusting

175g (6oz) unsalted butter, softened

175g (6oz) caster sugar

4 eggs

175g (6oz) ground almonds

1 tsp almond extract

175g (6oz) mincemeat

50g (2oz) flaked almonds

Thick cream, to serve

ROLL OUT THE PASTRY ON A FLOURED SURFACE and use it to line a 28cm (11in) flan tin (see page 11). Prick the base of the pastry with a fork. Chill the pastry case in the fridge for 10 minutes, then preheat the oven to 190°C (375°F), Gas Mark 5 and blind bake the pastry case for 25 minutes (see page 11). Remove and set aside, leaving the oven turned on.

IN A MIXING BOWL, cream together the butter and sugar until pale and fluffy. Beat in the eggs then add the ground almonds and almond extract. Mix until fully incorporated. Spread the mincemeat evenly in the cooked pastry case and top with the creamed mixture. Bake for 30–40 minutes, then sprinkle the flaked almonds onto the tart and put back in the oven for 5 minutes. Serve warm with thick cream.

Spiced winter fruit salad

SERVES 6

600g (1lb 5oz) mixed dried fruit, including apricots, pitted Agen prunes, pears, apples and figs
3 tbsp good-quality clear honey
½ tsp mixed spice
1 vanilla pod
1 tbsp fresh lemon juice
Good-quality vanilla ice cream or Greek yoghurt, to serve

PLACE THE DRIED FRUITS into a large saucepan and cover with 750ml (1 pint 6fl oz) cold water. Leave to soak for 2–3 hours.

ADD THE HONEY AND MIXED SPICE to the pan. Split the vanilla pod, scrape the seeds into the liquor and also add the pod. Mix well together, then bring to the boil and simmer for 15 minutes.

REMOVE THE PAN FROM THE HEAT, fish out the vanilla pod and discard. Add the lemon juice and leave to infuse. The fruit salad can be served warm or left to cool. Serve with vanilla ice cream or Greek yoghurt.

INDEX

221

THREE WAYS HOUSE HOTEL, in the beautiful countryside of the North Cotswolds, has been the home of The Pudding Club since it was first established in 1985. Pudding-lovers from all over the world have visited us to enjoy a pudding in Randall's Bar Brasserie, the buffet of puddings at Sunday lunch in the award-winning restaurant or to join in the fun at a unique meeting of The Pudding Club itself. Many choose to stay overnight in one of the seven pudding-themed bedrooms; after all where else could you sleep in a box of chocolates or under a dripping syrup sponge?

Our mission has been to preserve the heritage of the great British pudding. Please come along to enjoy a pudding or two and help us in our work:

THREE WAYS HOUSE HOTEL
Chapel Lane, Mickleton, Chipping Campden, Gloucestershire, GL55 6SB
Tel: 01386 438429,
Email: reception@puddingclub.com
www.puddingclub.com
www.threewayshousehotel.com

ACKNOWLEDGEMENTS

WE WOULD LIKE TO THANK everyone at Three Ways House Hotel for their energy and enthusiasm in making The Pudding Club the world-famous institution it is today and for their ideas and recipes, which helped to create this book. We are particularly grateful to the queen of puddings, Sheila Vincent, who has made many thousands of delicious puddings since 1995. Thanks too to Head Chef Mark and to Tom, Carl, Dan, Rachel and Peter's wife Jane who have all been a big help.

Thanks too to Sarah Lavelle, Smith & Gilmour, Ione Walder and everyone at Ebury.

Simon and Jill Coombe and Peter Henderson, The Pudding Club

THE
PUDDING CLUB
EST. 1985

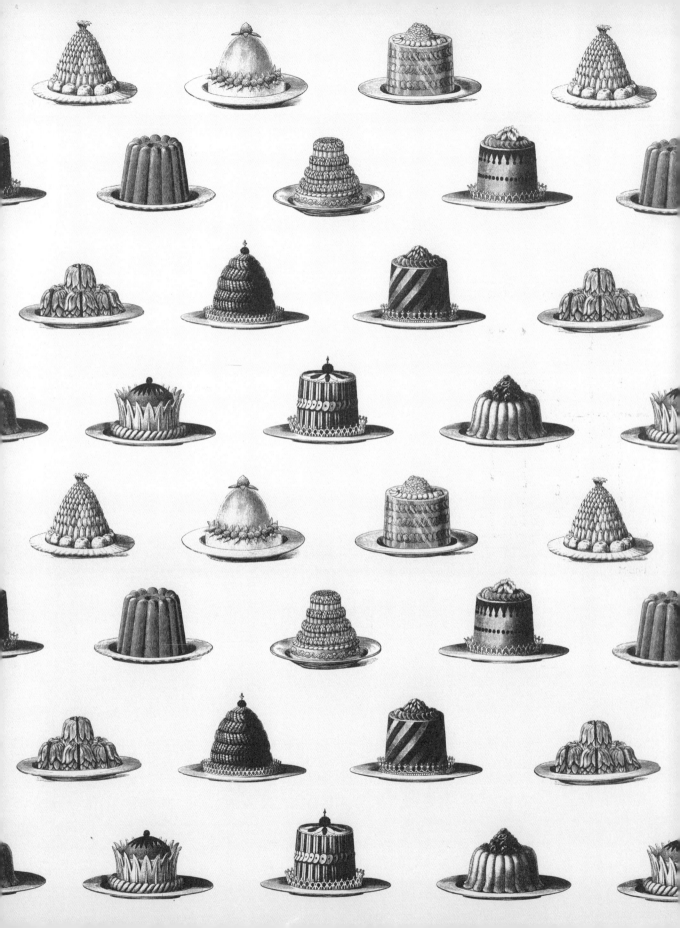